HIGH PERFORMANCE BRANCH BANKING

A Manager's Guide to Maximizing Branch Profitability

Dwight Ritter

IRWIN
Professional Publishing®
Chicago • London • Singapore

© Dwight S. Ritter, 1996

This publication is designed to provide accurate and authoritative information in regard to the subject matter covered. It is sold with the understanding that neither the author nor the publisher is engaged in rendering legal, accounting, or other professional service. If legal advice or other expert assistance is required, the services of a competent professional person should be sought.

From a Declaration of Principles jointly adopted by a Committee of the American Bar Association and a Committee of Publishers.

◤◥ **Times Mirror**
◣ **Higher Education Group**

Library of Congress Cataloging-in-Publication Data
Ritter, Dwight S.
    High performance branch banking: a manager's guide to maximizing branch profitability / Dwight Ritter.
       p. cm.
    Includes index.
    ISBN 1–55738–799–0
    1. Branch banks—Management.   I. Title.
HG1616.B7R583   1996
332.1'6—dc20   96–5641

Printed in the United States of America
1 2 3 4 5 6 7 8 9 0   3 2 1 0 9 8 7 6

This book is dedicated to my father,
Wayne Lockwood Ritter. 1908–1990.
He was turned down for a loan in 1946.
He never tried again.
He hated bankers ever since!
But I sure loved him.

CONTENTS IN BRIEF

CONTENTS

Chapter 4

Identifying the Small Business Customer   47

Chapter 5

Improving Sales Communications   55

Chapter 6

How to Ask Questions That Your Customer Wants to Answer   79

Chapter 7

Building a Sales Model   93

FOREWORD

When John Kenneth Galbraith once said, "banking may be the only profession from which no man fully recovers," he must have been thinking of those who have chosen to work only on the so-called *wholesale side* (business accounts) of commercial banking—which has certainly had its perilous ups and downs.

Lest there be any doubt concerning the long-term strength and viability of the *retail side* (individual accounts), the words of the implacable former Chief of Citicorp, Walter Wriston, are worth recalling: "70 percent of all capital formation in the U. S., over at least the next half century, will have its origin in *individual* and *household* earning power."

Yes, "retail banking" is very much alive and will surely flourish for perceptive practitioners for quite a long time to come. But the banking triumphs of the future will undoubtedly go to those who best understand, capture, and implement the finer points of author Ritter's *new approaches* for resourceful branch management, in the delivery of financial services to those same *households* to which Wriston refers.

Of the hundreds of banking books, journals, articles, and monographs that I have either read or written in my 40 years in the business, *High Performance Branch Banking* is, by a wide margin, the most penetrating and enlightening of all on the crucial *retail* side.

What I found most useful in this book includes:

- A revealing exposé of the predicament of overworked branch personnel who hunger to learn how to *run the branch,* before becoming involved in an *accountable sales effort;*
- A handy model for *time allocation* by the branch manager;
- A straightforward formula for assimilating *change;*
- $C = (D + V + S) > X$;
- The emerging *global economy;*
- The "soft" versus the "hard" sell;
- Assessing the *worth* of a new account;

- The folly of "smokestacking";
- Concerning "power structures";
- About *body language*—55 percent of communications;
- *Conflict* resolution;
- The invaluable *open-ended question* in needs-based selling;
- The dynamics of an effective *sales model;*
- Stimulating the *cross sale;*
- The *three categories* of products and services;
- Creating a *mental sales path;*
- Understanding the two ways business *makes money* (case studies);
- Achieving a "commitment to belonging" among the sales team;
- The pros and cons of "incentive compensation";
- *Managing* versus *leading*—a matter of blending; and
- *Solutions* to the three case studies, calculated to enlighten branch personnel.

In a word—make that two words—this timely work is *uniquely creative,* both as to content and format for those who will answer the crucial call for more effective branch banking for the nineties. These pages have invaluable insight that might otherwise require both too many years and much too much pain to discover independently.

> J. W. McLEAN
> Past-President Federal Advisory Council
> of the Federal Reserve System

PREFACE

Since the time of the publication of my first banking book, *Cross-Selling Financial Services* (New York: John Wiley Sons, 1988), I have become more involved in the process of implementing what people refer to as *a culture.* I was spending more and more time in the branches: talking with branch managers, filling in at a desk and selling, handling employee problems, and going to the main office and trying to convince executive management to do something different, to change.

At the same time, my company's involvement in branch banking outside of the United States has greatly expanded. We have worked with a number of major banks in Europe, the United Kingdom, and Ireland. I began to realize that the business cultures outside the United States greeted change and welcomed new ideas. More significantly, I noticed that foreign banks truly concentrate on the employees. In the United States, we say we do. But when times get tough, we forget them. The best example is that in an economic downturn U.S. firms cut their training budget. In many European businesses, they increase it and concentrate on increased productivity through making their employees more efficient. We simply do not put our money where our mouth is.

With the current changing environment in banking, both in the United States and abroad, branch productivity becomes an issue of great importance. You might say that it has always been important but we know, in truth, that is not so. I have spoken to numerous commercial bankers who scoff at retail banking as simply "a place for my commercial customers to do business."

And that was all well and good as long as our commercial loans and mortgages were "solid." Today we are finding out that the lending side of the balance sheet is not quite as easy as we thought. Growing problems in the area of lending force us to concentrate on more secure, smaller, consumer installment loans, conservative residential mortgages, and well-researched investments. Probably we will return to the good ole days of freewheeling lending. We always seem to do that somehow. But we have learned a lesson: Retail branch banking, in and of itself, if approached properly, can be the backbone of a financial institution

This book is about structure. It is a how-to guide for the retail branch banker. The research that has gone into this text reflects the input of literally thousands of bankers from all over the United States, Europe, and the Caribbean. I hope it will become required reading for every branch manager.

My approach requires a highly structured, long-term look. This means questioning some of your implanted thoughts and opinions about banking. Surely we can't assume that profits will come from a couple of sales training classes. That would be as naive as assuming that profits could come from a couple of good-sized loans. Wouldn't it?

ACKNOWLEDGMENTS

Naturally when approaching a project such as writing a book, one relies heavily on other people for information, guidance, and support. Unfortunately there are not enough pages to list the names of individuals and banks who participated in our several mailed research questionnaires. For those who helped, I offer my heartfelt thanks.

The ideas presented in this book are a result of my involvement with many financial institutions, both national and international. My close involvement with some of these banks enabled me to *get inside* and talk to the people and find out *why*. I learned about the characteristics of a corporate champion. I learned the breadth of variables that affect a sales culture and an immense level of politics that invariably slows down the process and costs more money. I learned about the dollars and cents—pounds and pence—issues that cloud branch profitability. And I learned how banks make money.

MARTHA'S A FRIEND OF MINE

Martha's a friend of mine. She's a branch manager for a large regional bank. Fifteen years ago, her bank was a little savings bank. She managed one of three branches. Then they were bought by a bigger bank, which in turn was bought by the present bank. Needless to say, Martha's been around the track a few times!

Martha and I were talking in her office amid the phone ringing, tellers interrupting for check authorization, and customers giving her dirty looks because of long lines. For 10 years, her branch administrator or retail banking head has been sending her to sales classes. We were talking about the number of different sales classes she's been through: seven in all.

"BAI, AID, BMA . . . You name it, I've been through it. I did PSS in 1973," Martha said.

"Do you really like to sell?" I asked.

"You want the truth?" she asked.

"Of course," I replied.

"I rarely sell."

"But, Martha, you're the bank's sales guru."

She smirked. "I'm serious," I said.

"I am serious," she said as she leaned back in her chair. "One, I don't have the time to sell; and, two, I'm really threatened by a structured, organized, accountable sales effort."

"But I thought . . . "

"You thought that I brought in a lot of business for the bank. That's the rumor."

"Yeah."

"Well, I have and I haven't." She leaned forward, resting her arms on her cluttered desk. "My husband John has a great job. We socialize a lot. I've lived in this town for 20 years. My kids went to school here. I was president of the PTA. The only business I brought in has been personal friends. I didn't ask for their business. It was totally their idea. A couple of our friends own some pretty fair-sized businesses. And they told Art [the bank president] what a great salesperson I was. Honestly, I know what a salesperson does. I've been through too many sales classes. And I know I don't do it."

"Wow! You mean you're the star salesperson because you're lucky?"

"Right. But I'm not complaining and I wouldn't tell anyone else."

"I'm flabbergasted."

"Dwight, here's what you and people in executive management don't understand. Branch managers don't have time to leave their branch and call on customers, follow up with letters, send them press clippings, call them up to chat, send 'em birthday cards. We just don't have the time!"

"Oh come on, Martha."

"I'm serious. Let's be logical here. Assume you have a job to do. For argument's sake, you've got 50 parts to your job. It's taken you 10 years to fit those 50 parts into a realistic 40-hour workweek. OK?"

"I'm with you."

"Now, your boss comes along and says, 'Here's 10 more parts you'll need to add to your job.' That makes 60 parts. How am I gonna get my job done? Remember, my boss did not say, 'Here's 10 new parts, I'm taking away 10 old parts.' He didn't say, 'Here's another employee to do those 10 parts.' He just added 10 parts. After all, I'm the manager. I'm supposed to figure out how to get these things done. It's not Art's problem. I'm the manager.

"Now here's where the rubber hits the road. I can't figure out how to add those 10 parts to my job! Period."

"You mean you don't want to," I interrupt.

"There might be some truth to that; but no one is telling me how to reorganize."

"So you're telling me that if I expect you to undertake a serious, accountable sales effort, I have to teach you how to manage your branch."

"You got it."

TODD MAKES ME NERVOUS

The first time I met Todd I was particularly suspicious. His desk was spotless . . . not empty . . . spotless. Well-organized. Immediately, I didn't feel comfortable around him. My desk looks like an unorganized confetti convention. Todd looked real good. My shirt smelled.

"Tell me, Todd," I said, shifting in my chair. "Do you sell?"

"Absolutely," he said with a broad Tom Cruise smile.

Now, I knew I had him. "How many new accounts do you call on each month?"

"Seven, actually," he said, thumbing through a red Economist Diary, "nine this month. I have to make three sales from seven calls. I wasn't going to make my quota on seven. So I made nine to get three."

"That must take some time," I stammered.

"Not really."

"What do you mean, 'not really'?" I was getting a little tired of his cockiness.

"It averages out to a day and a half per week out of the branch."

"A day and a half. Geez, who runs the branch?" I asked.

"Well, I have Marilyn out there. She's my assistant. Used to be a CSR [customer service representative]. I fought like crazy to make her an assistant so I could give her some lending authority. That young man over there is Billy Fores. He's a part-time CSR. Beth Cervantes is my head teller and she supervises three full-time and two part-time tellers."

"Yeah," I nodded, "but who runs the branch?" I asked.

"They do."

"Come on," I persisted. "Who does your morning overdraft returns?"

"For the most part, Marilyn. Sometimes it's Beth."

"I thought you told me Beth was a head teller."

"That's right."

"What's she doing authorizing overdraft returns?"

"Hey, she knows the customers better than I do. And a $20 overdraft return is a waste of my time. I should be out of the branch working on small-to-medium-size businesses, not slaving over $20 overdrafts."

"Uhmm," I agreed, he made a lot of sense. "What about taking the bags out of the night depository and opening the vault and bringing up the machines and proofing the ATM cards, verifying traveler's checks, . . . and stuff like that?"

He chuckled. "I haven't done that kind of stuff in years. Honestly, Mr. River"

"Ritter," I corrected.

"Honestly, Mr. Ritter, I'm a salesman. Marilyn is too. So is Billy. They do internal selling. We meet formally every Saturday morning to see how they are doing against the goals we set. I work with customers. I cross sell. I handle the real bears who insult Marilyn. I plan my cold calling. I organize my leads and I diligently make myself an integral part of this community.

"Running the branch is something everyone needs to learn how to do. So why should I do it all?"

I wondered how I was going to help this bank.

SPINNING TIRES TO HEAR THEM SQUEAL

Twenty years ago I worked at a bank in the southeast part of the United States. The branch manager was one who, throughout the day, would emit slight audible gasps of breath. "Whew," she would whisper—over and over again, all day long—mostly when one of her tellers or customer service reps would be within hearing distance. She would always walk very fast from one location to the next, going, "Whew," with her hair and dress flowing out behind her like walking into the wind, taking large strides, her arms swinging. From the very beginning I was in awe of this woman.

"This is one busy branch manager," I would think.

Even though I was a consultant working at the bank, trying to determine their level of sales sophistication, she insisted that everyone in her bank had to chip in, especially the consultants.

"You've never really worked in a bank before," she said, aiming her eyes and nose carefully at me.

"Well actually, I have. I . . ."

She interrupted. "I mean like this branch. We are terribly understaffed! Each year this bank comes up with some new gimmick and expects me to figure out how to make it happen. "If you are going to be working with us, you will have to pull your weight."

"Oh, absolutely," I nodded in a submissive and concerned way. "I would expect to do everything everyone else is doing. I don't want to disrupt your branch."

"Well," she huffed. "The damage is done. We will just have to work a little harder. I will ask you to do loan apps. Do you know how to do that?"

"You mean just taking applications from customers?"

"Of course."

"I'll be happy to do that if you will just get me started the first time."

"Well, all right," she said, inhaling deeply and rolling her eyes in their muted mascara sockets.

After two weeks, I began writing down the tasks that she performed. Ashamedly, I even began eavesdropping on her telephone conversations. You see, I sincerely needed to know how she was able to juggle the myriad tasks that she had to perform. I hope I never have to be a branch manager, I would think to myself, too much work. Too much responsibility.

Monday: unlocked the vault. Told Mary to bring up the machines. Went into her office and got on the phone. Laughed a lot. Overheard her say, "No. He didn't really say that," and she laughed some more. Saw me watching. Told me to get her some coffee. Cremora, three sugars, stir well. Gerri told me she was working on a maintenance request. A customer came in and spent 45 minutes with her. She had two phone calls. Told Mary to watch the branch for her. She had to make a call as part of her officer call program. She returned after lunch. Handled two more customers who were obviously friends. Told Gerri she would have to take the insurance credit reports off the tracking sheets for her. Tidied up her office; apparently she lost something and was looking for it. Took one call from her daughter. Called her husband. Oversaw the balancing out at the end of the day. Turned the lights out when she left. Whew!

Once, at the end of the day, I asked her, "Is this a busy branch?"

"You mean you can't tell?" she replied almost hysterically.

"Well," I fumbled and stammered. "It appears to be, but is it?"

"Of course, it is."

"Uhh," I ventured gingerly, "How many transactions do we do here on a monthly basis?"

"Now how am I supposed to know that? Do you expect me to stand around behind my tellers and count?"

"Well no. I just thought maybe the main office would send you those figures."

"Well they don't. And thank the good Lord for that because I wouldn't have time to look at them."

"You mean you don't really have any idea how busy you are or how much money you are making?"

Then she addressed me as, "Mr. Smarty Pants." I guess I deserved it. She got rid of me in three days. She told the branch administrator I was disrupting her branch.

That was 20 years ago, after all.

CHAPTER 1

Managing Today's Retail Branch

A HISTORY OF BRANCH BANKING

The role of the branch manager in today's bank has changed in many ways. Let's reflect back a little and remember that role 30 years ago, when branch managers functioned as chief operating officers of their branches. They did so because 30 years ago the retail operations of most banks were decentralized; that is, all of the paperwork and account data was kept in the branches. Stacks and stacks of boxes were filled with files of customer information. Under the counters, in the basement, carefully organized in beige cardboard; many with handwritten notes on the contents. Some files were stacked behind the teller counters for easier access. I am told by branch managers of 40 years ago that they specially identified some boxes of frequent customers—those were kept behind the teller counters. There were other boxes of not-so-frequent customers—those were kept in the basement, alphabetized for quick reference.

That was 40 years ago in the United States. There are still some banks in this country that maintain a lot of the manual filing systems of yesteryear. In many countries where centralized operations have not happened, branches still function with manual systems. For example, in Ireland many banks are decentralized from an operational point of view. Under the customer service counters, there are boxes of customer files. Behind the teller cages, more boxes of files. This is in the process of changing.

Branch managers in Ireland still operate as chief operating officers. They are paid more than U.S. branch managers because their branches are physically bigger with more people due to a built-in back-room operation in every branch. They also function as the senior lending officers within the community, and some hire but do not fire. Due to Irish unemployment at approximately 18 percent, hiring isn't that much of an issue. In Massachusetts, where unemployment is at 4 percent, hiring is a major issue. So Massachusetts banks centralize their hiring even though the entry-level workforce in banking is decaying due to low unemployment and the invasion of the peak time workforce (the PEATYs).

Americans think this decentralized approach to retail banking is antiquated. But is it? Different countries have different cultures. The Irish are raised differently than Americans—no better, no worse. Different. In Ireland, this decentralized approach to operations is the result of a heavily savings-oriented society. The United States is a consumption-oriented society. We live in a world of checking accounts and other spending vehicles to pay for our BMWs, designer jeans, Tissot rock watches, brass garden decorations, ad nauseam. Ireland, as an example, offers primarily savings vehicles. From time to time, it has tried offering NOW accounts, but the market has not been ready for it. Irish banks offer checking accounts (called current accounts) in their branches, although they make up only 16 percent of their new accounts. In the United States, checking accounts make up 42 percent of new accounts. Up until 1990, building societies (the U.S. equivalent of an S&L or mortgage company) did not even offer checking (current) accounts. In 1990, building societies began offering checking accounts and other traditional consumer banking products. Irish banking is changing as the whole world seems to shrink.

What this illustrates is that banks, like other businesses, operate in response to their markets. As technology grows and management skills become heightened, businesses must experiment with change. Because of our vast computer capabilities, *a logical cost-savings area for banks has been to centralize the operational aspects of a bank.* Ireland, too, has already started to centralize their operations. Europe is facing a similar consumer banking dilemma: high salaries, highly operations-oriented, high unemployment, growing economy, and transitional consumer habits.

U.S. branch managers operate in a totally centralized operational environment. The branches tend to be physically smaller than those of the United Kingdom, Europe, and Australia. U.S. branch managers do not have the operational responsibilities found in international banks; consequently, their managerial tasks are fewer.

U.S. retail bankers have an abundance of services and personnel demands. Additionally, many U.S. branch managers still operate their branches by spending 80 percent of their time on operational issues. Yet their operational tasks have been diminished manyfold since the sixties. From a global point of view, U.S. branch managers have fewer operational responsibilities than foreign branch managers, yet spend less time calling on small businesses.

THE PATH FOR PROFITS

Businesses make money by increasing income and/or reducing expenses. Simplistic but true. Banks have urged their customer-contact staff to sell, and they have downsized the branch system, allowing fewer employees per customer. As shareholders put more pressure on management for profits, they began looking at creating more sales for fewer dollars. By buying another bank, the buying bank could buy more customers. They could process those customers through their own operations system, eliminating the need for two operations departments. So the buying bank increased its sales and decreased its expenses.

Then we realized that on many Tuesdays and Wednesdays our branch personnel were not that busy. Financially we fantasized about having them work only when it was busy; that is, paying them only when it was busy. And thus the birth of the peak time worker (the PEATY). When employees quit or were terminated, we were given a PEATY to replace them.

If you were part of the executive management of a bank and responsible to your shareholders, you would do exactly the same. The result is that today's branch managers require behavior-based management skills that few of them were taught or understand. So today's branch manager is not equipped to manage today's branch efficiently and effectively.

The Branch Manager

The branch manager of the twenty-first century will have to be high on leadership skills and understand the behavioral processes involved in motivating a workforce.

To realistically understand the branch manager's role in our changing industry, let's look at the overall responsibilities as diagrammed in

Figure 1–1. This will give you a chance to view, graphically, what the branch manager does! For simplicity, we have divided the overall responsibilities into four categories: sales/service, planning, human resource development, and operations.

Sales/service

In a branch, there are two different kinds of selling: internal selling and external selling. When you function as a platform person working with a customer who comes in asking for a product and you provide him with that product and another product, then you have cross sold. You cross sell the second product, the third, and so on. We refer to cross selling as internal selling. The first product that you provide to the customer comes under the heading of customer service, not sales! We cover this in greater depth in Chapter 8 on cross selling.

Depending on the size of your branch and your inclination to delegate responsibilities, you can spend a lot or a little time with customers. We do know that the more time you spend selling and servicing, the more knowledge you have to provide better coaching and guidance to your staff. If you think you are not any good at selling, you probably shouldn't be a branch manager in today's sales-oriented banking environment.

External selling occurs when you leave your branch on a regular basis and make sales calls on small businesses within your branch marketing area. Incidentally, this book is about external selling.

FIGURE 1–1

The Duties of the Branch Manager

A major portion of this category is the routine day-to-day servicing of customers—solving customer's problems, making exceptions, handling complaints, or balancing their checkbooks.

Planning

Planning is a function you either do frequently or have organized yourself to do weekly or monthly. Your main office makes this planning area critical. If you are part of a major branch network, this area can become all-encompassing and take away from your duties as a people manager and customer liaison. For the purpose of this time management analysis, planning includes intrabranch meetings; new product planning; overtime; and budgeting—especially sales statistics, cross sales ratios, and goal setting. Remember that numbers are your way of documenting your progress. Your management needs quantitative evidence.

Human Resource Development

As a manager, you spend time with your people, coaching, resolving personality disputes, making follow-through reminders, training, and counseling. Additionally, this involves all of your people management functions, such as creating and executing branch events, or taking your customer service reps out for a well-deserved dinner.

Operations

Operations has been referred to as stuck vault management. In my many visits to branch managers, I continually ask them what percentage of their time is spent on operational issues. They ask what I mean by operational issues?

"Oh, things like time spent on your stuck vault."

"Oh, that kind of operational thing," they reply immediately.

Following are the 10 most prevalent routine operational tasks a U.S. branch manager has. These tasks also include phone calls and memos.

1. Prepare the morning overdraft returns.

2. Take the bags out of the night depository.

3. Open the vault and bring up the machines.

4. Prepare the fair-housing log.

5. Proof the ATM cards.

6. Verify the traveler's checks.

7. Fill out grounds and maintenance requests.

8. Type the telephone notes.

9. Prepare the weekly loan-tracking sheets.

10. Prepare the insurance credit reports.

WHAT YOUR CONTEMPORARIES DO

We surveyed branch managers across the country in 1982 and again in late 1995 and grouped their responses by category. When asked how branch managers spend their time, here's what we got:

1982	1995
Sales/service, 14%	Sales/service, 39%
Planning, 13%	Planning, 11%
Human resource, 19%	Human resource, 21%
Operations, 54%	Operations, 29%

I spend several days each month with branch managers and have have analyzed those skills of good branch managers—as well as those inefficiencies of bad branch managers. The one variable that makes a good branch manager good and a bad one bad is flexibility. Can you sell when it is time to sell? Can you fill in on the teller line, analyze numbers, conduct a sales meeting, argue with senior management? It doesn't mean doing them all well—only doing them all.

If you own a bank and someone tells you that your staff needs to be more sales-oriented, and you look into what your branch managers are doing, you will find a vast area for improvement if your branch managers are spending 50 percent of their time on operational tasks. Managers who are good at training and developing the staff, can easily delegate operational tasks.

Now the issue is simple: If you are supposed to spend more time selling, who is going to do what you're doing now? The fact is, many branch managers spend as much as 80 percent of their time on operational problems. Those branch managers find it very difficult to participate in the current worldwide shift in a branch manager's responsibilities.

Some branch managers spend a lot of time inside the branch with customers. A customer-sensitive branch manager can spend 30 to 40 percent of her time working with customers: account servicing, opening new accounts, a little cross selling, and putting out fires. But not really selling, not building the external sale into the everyday work schedule.

Clearly, what needs to happen is a redefining of the tasks and responsibilities in the branch. Try this exercise: Write down the names of the people in your branch who perform the tasks listed in Figure 1–1. See if there might be a better way of delegating responsibilities.

When one really thinks about it, almost all of those routine operational tasks can be delegated. Even if you are part of a small branch with no assistant; or part of a small branch with no assistant and no CSR. To whom do you delegate? To whoever is next in line.

Many branch managers have told me that they are forbidden to delegate certain tasks. Other branch managers who sell tell me they delegate a lot, so they can be with customers and prospective customers.

"How do you delegate overdraft returns?" a branch manager will ask.

"Does your assistant branch manager have lending authority?" I ask.

"Louise? Well, limited. But, honestly, I wouldn't trust her to approve my kid's allowance."

"How about your CSRs?" I persist.

"Well, only Brenda has limited authority. Tom doesn't; thank God! Mary Ellen doesn't even know what it is."

"Could Brenda do some of the returns?" I wonder.

"Not any better than Louise."

"Sounds to me like you need to teach Louise and Brenda about overdraft returns. You know, make up some guidelines, some rules. You gotta teach them."

"When?" she asks, hands on hips with a slight, knowing snarl on her face.

My fictitious branch manager is being human, she has gotten into comfortable habits. Just like you, she has a fairly comfortable pattern going in her life. Then change threatens that comfortable pattern. We guard our patterns psychologically. We guard them by coming up with reasons why we cannot make the change.

Clearly, the branch manager (1) could have delegated some or all of the overdraft returns, (2) could have provided training to Louise and Brenda, (3) could have requested that Louise or Brenda be transferred, or (4) could have recommended that Louise or Brenda be fired.

Our branch manager had several options. If you are a good manager, you have analyzed your job carefully and you have weighed each of your responsibilities in terms of which ones you can delegate and what it would take for you to delegate certain responsibilities.

You should know how many hours on average you spend in an operational mode. Use the following chart to make some calculated guesses. Within your particular bank or geographic area, there might be other important operational tasks that are not listed. So list them. Analyze them. Write them on a board. Have all your employees sit down at the end of the day and go through those tasks with you. Ask them which ones they could do.

If you are serious about fitting into a sales culture, you must find the time to make sales calls outside of the branch. You must find time to cross sell inside the branch. You must find time to operate as a sales manager for your branch.

The operational area is most easily delegated. How many hours each week do you spend in operational duties?

Operational Functions	Hours per Week
1. Prepare the morning overdraft returns.	_____
2. Take the bags out of the night depository.	_____
3. Open the vault and bring up the machines.	_____
4. Prepare the fair-housing log.	_____
5. Proof the ATM cards.	_____
6. Verify the traveler's checks.	_____
7. Fill out grounds and maintenance requests.	_____
8. Type the telephone notes.	_____
9. Prepare the weekly loan-tracking sheets.	_____
10. Prepare the insurance credit reports.	_____

If you are one of those managers who is thoroughly convinced that there is absolutely no time to sell or manage a sales effort, you will be struggling through the next decade of retail banking. That goes for the branch managers from Cork, Ireland, to Kansas City, Curacao, Canberra, Kyoto, Caracas, Copenhagen, Coimbra, and Cologne. The role of the branch manager is changing. Branch banking is becoming customer-driven versus operations-driven. When the customer drives an industry, the providers to that industry must constantly analyze the needs of that customer and inform the customer how they have satisfied his needs; that is, they become more customer-sensitive, focusing on the customer rather than focusing on the product.

Because of a rapidly shifting economic global environment that affects retail banking, we must rethink our jobs. Here is the essence of the thinking process:

Do I manage when I am not selling?
or
Do I sell when I am not managing?

The process is one of priorities. Are you totally sales-oriented? Is selling built into your management style? How often do you have a structured sales meeting with your tellers, assistant managers, customer service reps? You should meet once a week for five minutes.

How many hours per week are you out of the office making calls on prospective clients or cultivating existing relationships? Our research show that a retail, sales-oriented, large branch has its branch manager out of the office one and a half days each week—a day and a half of networking, selling, and cultivating. Some branch managers are out of the office two days each week, primarily selling mortgages and working with realtors; others are out making calls on small retailers.

The branch manager who is often out needs to have an efficient backup system in the branch. Who will run the branch while the branch manager is out?

How do I delegate?

How do I find the time to decide how I delegate?

Who do I train so I can delegate?

How do I find the time to train so I can delegate?

When do I decide to find the time to decide how I delegate?

Meet with your staff to write down those tasks that might be delegated and discuss them.

There are a wide variety of branches, in terms of size, decor, or staff. By now, you have probably said, "That sure doesn't apply to me." Some doesn't, but the knowledge does. So let's discuss the different kinds of branches.

Many branch managers know a lot about their branches while others know very little. That knowledge is directly dependent on the senior management of the bank; some want the branch managers to know a lot and others don't want them to know anything. You should know some rules of thumb about banking regarding dollars and people and geography. For many of you, this might be old hat, and for some, new hat.

If you are sitting in your branch reading this book and occasionally peering over the top of the page to check the lobby and circuitously watch your teller line, and your branch consists of two full-time tellers and yourself, you are probably managing a ± $15 million branch. It isn't a big branch. That doesn't mean it isn't important. Importance depends on how your branch stacks up to the other branches within a three-mile radius. If there are only three other banks within that marketing area and they're all the same size, your branch is important and competitive. We developed Figure 1–2 for those branch managers who often wonder how big their branches are and/or how many people they should have. "Are we really too busy?"

F I G U R E   1–2

Branch Employee Efficiency

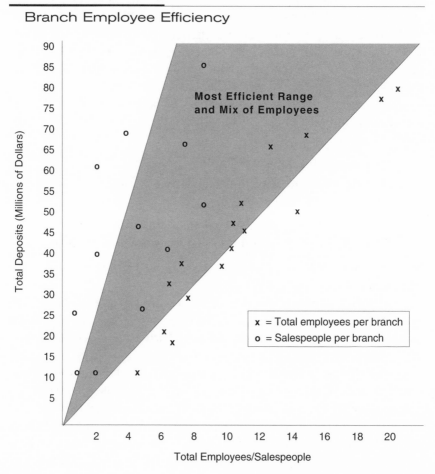

We did a random sampling of branches in the United States and plotted (1) deposits, (2) total employees, and (3) total trained sales employees. We found there is a most efficient level of employees per branch. The shaded area of the chart shows that level of efficiency. Plot your branch and count your employees. Or, if you don't know the size of your branch in deposits, count your employees, go up to the diagonal line, and then cross to the left. That deposit size should be close to what your branch has.

That should tell you something about your branch. It varies, depending on whether you are in a major city or in a rural setting. This chart has very little to do with profits, because most banks still view their branch structure by total deposits rather than sales. However, every year more banks begin treating their branches as profit centers and measuring sales and expenses so the branch manager can truly understand how these impact the bottom line. Ever so slowly our branches are turning into independent retail outlets.

MEASURING BRANCH PROFITABILITY

Some progressive retail banks measure their branches on their own return on equity (ROE). ROE is simply after-tax profits divided by equity. Many traditional banks measure their progress on return on assets (ROA). ROE is based on strength; ROA is based on size.

Some banks have developed realistic sales values for products. For example, they calculate that a particular branch's average checking account is worth $58.10. So every checking account in that particular branch has a sales value. If my branch opens 100 checking accounts, I can say it did $5,810 in sales. Banks that utilize this approach generally take a total number of checking accounts in the branch and factor in such variables as the average daily balance, the average length of time the account stays in the branch, and the average gross spread of the bank. They come up with a dollar value on each account and, to offset that income, they develop transaction expenses. This method is extremely easy for branch personnel to understand, because it is simpler to report dollar values to which a CSR can relate.

At present, we can learn something from existing numbers. Many large accounting firms, consultants, and some banks have settled on a hypothetical break-even point, determined by taking a percentage of deposits and calling it expenses. Or perhaps more correctly, taking existing known expenses (rent, salaries, benefits, utilities) and determining their percentage of deposits.

In the early eighties, 10 percent of a branch's total deposits were supposed to be expenses. Today, it is actually less than 3 percent. Breakeven, based on deposits, is not an indication of profitability.

As a branch manager of the twenty-first century, you must know the numbers. Authorities are always presenting new kinds of numbers. We are learning how to calculate the market share of our branches and branch share in a geographic area. We are learning to conceptualize that banks make money by bringing in deposits and giving out loans. The efficient interplay of those two functions controls profits in retail banking.

> Barry Levinson manages a branch in the Midwest. He has five full-time tellers, one assistant branch manager, and one CSR. Barry knows his deposits increased by 12 percent over last year. He also is painfully aware that he has no new people.
>
> There is a new sales program in the bank. His assistant branch manager and his CSR both are being tracked. Barry is supposed to manage their productivity. Also he is supposed to make two external calls each week. Just two. He has to fill out a form for each. He likes to do his calls, but his branch is suffering. His assistant like to cross sell and spend time with the customers. So does Barry. The operational aspects of the branch are going to hell in a handbasket!

A PREPARATORY LOOK AT BRANCHES

Branches evolve and grow or evolve and die. Their staffing and size have become a matter of record and, therefore, fairly predictable.

Tiny Branch: $10 Million

A tiny branch is the under $10 million branch. That branch might have one full-time and one PEATY teller and a branch manager. The branch manager functions as the customer service representative, branch manager, fill-in teller, and secretary. If we ask this branch manager to spend one day each week away from the branch, who will run the branch? Can we dump more responsibilities on the head teller? Can that teller be multi-skilled and perhaps trained for management? At this size, you fix things when they are broken and function as order taker, and sometimes sales-person, with your customers.

Small Branch: $18 Million

The small branch is at that stage of development when you add a desk in the lobby. Then you put in a request for someone to sit at that desk. As your branch grows from $10 to $12 million, up to about $18 million, you are struggling with management because customers are trying to open accounts but you don't have the staff, time, or facilities to help them properly. So you ask management for help. In the meantime, you open new accounts at teller windows. You get an additional teller. You try to identify which tellers can open new basic checking and savings accounts. You improvise and learn shortcuts. At this size and this kind of staffing, you still must do operational tasks and sales.

Medium Branch: $25 Million

At about $20 to $25 million and up to $30 million, a branch starts looking like a branch. You have a CSR (maybe two) and five tellers; three are PEATYs. From a management point of view, you find that you must delegate responsibilities. This is when you realistically start looking through your operational tasks and balancing them against your customer/human resource tasks. This is when you can decide which way you will go, operations or sales.

This is a critical size for a branch. From a management point of view, you must start looking at your branch more conceptually. That means you must start breaking the duties of the branch into broad categories, such as

1. Operations/planning/human resource development
2. Internal sales/customer service
3. External sales

Theoretically, 66 percent of your job should be sales and service. As a branch manager of a $25 million branch, you can begin that transformation. At this size, you should have enough people to assume most of your operational duties.

Good-Sized Branch: $40 Million

In a good-sized branch, which, is today's average, you begin to see an economy of scale in your operational tasks: that is, as your branch deposits grow, your operational tasks do not grow proportionately. Your need for more people requires you to develop some behavioral management skills. And isn't it amusing that no one has ever taught them to you?

As you work your way up the organizational ladder, you gradually assume some managerial tasks. You learn them from the people who managed you. Suddenly, someone comes along and says, "OK. Be a manager." Now you're expected to know what to do. Most banks in the United States do not equip their branch managers with management training skills in the area of dealing with human behavior. If you manage a $40 to 60 million branch, understanding human behavior either makes you or breaks you. You can end up spending so much time being a policeman or parent that selling or operational tasks fall by the wayside.

Delegating emotional squabbles is difficult. Delegating employee involvement is difficult. Delegating employee coaching is difficult. So your decision with this size branch is not so much operational as it is human resource development. You've got enough people to delegate almost all of the operational tasks. You should think about clearing your plate so you can sell and manage salespeople.

Big Branch: $90+ Million

Managing a big branch is like running a large business. Your level of success directly depends on how you bring along your staff, cultivating new branch managers and salespeople. There is so much management in a big branch that you might look back on the amount of hands-on operational tasks you did in a $15 million branch and laugh.

If you haven't been able to organize yourself and your branch to allow for a major external sales effort, you shouldn't be managing a branch this size. You as well as your assistant branch managers should be out of the branch getting actively involved in your business community, cultivating leads, and making sales presentations. Additionally, you should be grooming one or more of your CSRs as external salespersons.

So it all boils down to reorganizing your work as you grow and as times change. You should not be managing your branch the same way you did four years ago.

Figure 1–3 allows you to look at your branch in terms of tasks. Across the top are spaces for you to write in the names of your personnel. As you can see, there are two areas for filling in spaces. One area is present tasks and the other is revised tasks. Fill in the spaces where certain

FIGURE 1-3

Employees' Tasks

Employees

Present Tasks **Revised Tasks**

Tasks

Teller tasks
Customer service tasks
  Account opening
  Cross selling
  Customer servicing
  External selling
Management tasks
  Account opening
  Cross selling
  Customer servicing
  External selling
  Weekly/monthly organizing
  Budgeting
  Meetings
  Employee coaching/counseling
  Branch events
Routine operational tasks
  Morning overdraft returns
  Removal of bags from night depository
  Opening vault
  Bringing up machines
  Fair-housing log
  Proofing ATM cards
  Verifying traveler's checks
  Grounds and maintenance requests
  Telephone notes
  Weekly loan-tracking sheets
  Weekly sales-tracking sheets
  Insurance credit reports

21

employees accomplish certain tasks. Under revised tasks fill in the chart again. A positive exercise here is to prepare this same chart on a flip chart. At a staff meeting, have the entire staff help you fill in both parts. This creates discussion and most certainly an awareness by your staff of what it means to manage a branch.

Chapter 13 has specific techniques to use in more effectively running your branch. It is purposely positioned toward the end of the book so we could provide basic information first. If you disagree, turn to Chapter 13!

S U M M A R Y

1. The role of the branch manager in today's bank has changed in many ways. Today's branch manager must learn to operate as a manager of the twenty-first century, by being in tune with current managerial techniques and styles.

2. Bank administration has changed considerably, putting much of the administrative side of retail banking into operations centers, thus taking a lot of the paperwork out of the branches.

3. How today's branches are organized.

4. According to a recent survey, branch managers allocate their time accordingly: sales/service, 39 percent; planning, 11 percent; human resource development, 21 percent; and operations, 29 percent.

5. A branch manager should meet with her staff to discuss sales once a week for five minutes.

6. Our research shows that a truly retail, sales-oriented, large branch of a bank has its branch manager out of the office one and a half days each week.

7. A tiny branch—about $10 million: The manager must do it all.

8. A small branch—$18 million: The manager begins the search for an internal sales person.

9. A medium branch—$25 million: The manager learns to manage a sales and service effort. He becomes more conceptual.

10. A good-sized branch—$40 million: The manager begins to manage "fires" and participate in the positioning of employees.

11. A big branch—$90+ million: The manager must rely heavily on her staff. She must learn how to cultivate new managers.

CHAPTER 2

Changes in Tokyo Affect Banks in Toledo and Timbuktu

The first time that I wrote this chapter, I decided that it would be the first chapter. It's about our country's business and economic plight, why we are in the shape we are in. Look at what's happening in banking today: bad loans, the shrinking residential mortgage market, increased expenses, and on and on. So I decided to start out the entire premise of learning about sales by explaining why we need to redo our priorities and become proactive (even aggressive) in our pursuit of banking business.

As I began to learn more and more about retail banking and the branch system, it became evident that the most important thing to do was to acknowledge the ongoing dispute with regard to branch managers not having the time to effectively pursue a retail sales environment. Then, if the branch managers were still reading, I would lay out the total rationale for change.

This chapter is about change. Why change? What brought on this need for change, especially when branch managers finally figured out how to run their branches smoothly?

CHANGE

1946, or so—that's the beginning point important to U.S. business. With the end of World War II and the reconstruction of Japan, an entire era of business and economics began.

The Japanese had lost the war. Their industrial empire was demolished by Allied bombing, especially by the atomic bomb. Their morale was at an all-time low. The Japanese people have experienced highs and lows for thousands of years. Regrouping for the Japanese has been a way of life.

On the other side of the Pacific Ocean was the United States. We have never had to regroup. We were and are young. Our economy has experienced steady growth and leveling. Looking at industrial production or wholesale price indexes, you find that (while fluctuating) the U.S. economy has continued to grow or remained level. Economically, we thrived during the War of 1812, the Civil War, and World War I. And we had our hard times in the early 1800s, 1858, the late 1870s, and the Great Depression. From 1863 to 1944, we had 20 recessions. From 1944 to present, we have had eight. From a global point of view, our growing pains were minimal.

We've been lucky these past 250 years! Up to 1914, we were in a learning phase, so we were continually changing. By 1914 the United States was the major world power. From 1914 to the end of World War II, we adjusted to the times. We were the big guys on the block. We didn't need to change. By the early fifties, we were learning how to control our economy and we were recognized worldwide as the leader in "making good things that worked real well."

Those of you in your fifties can recall those marvelous days of old when you received Christmas toys that didn't work from your parents. That was before batteries, when toys had to be wound up. They worked once or twice before the springs got messed up. The seams of toys came loose, and in a matter of minutes, some of the internal parts would fall out. We would be disgusted. Upon turning the toys over, we could always read where it came from. "Made in Japan." Gaads!

In the early fifties, Made in Japan meant poor quality, inferior, cheap, no good, ad nauseam. There were no Toyotas, Hondas, Mitsubishis, or Nissans in the good old USA. As a matter of fact, the few cars in Japan in the early fifties were American.

In the fifties, the best products in the world—that is, the ones that worked the best, looked the best, and were reasonably priced—were invariably made in the United States. We invented them, made them, and marketed them better than anyone in the world. Almost 100 percent of U.S. patents were granted to U.S. inventors.

One of those patents granted to a U.S. inventor was for a videocassette recorder. Ampex and an English company filed for that patent. They made the first videocassette recorder, priced it at just over $50,000, and determined that there just wasn't a market for those things. So they sold it to Sony, chuckling over the deal they just pulled off.

Look at the chart in Figure 2–1. Even though it is fairly nebulous, its true intent is extremely accurate. One of the world's leading experts in quality often uses this chart to illustrate how over time Japan caught and passed the United States in quality output. And for the sake of this chapter, let's define quality output as "a nation's ability to make good things that work real well." My definitions throughout this book are going to drive sophisticated businesspersons crazy.

Note a couple of dates in Figure 2–1. One is 1972, when Japan actually surpassed the United States in quality output. That is when Japanese imports into the United States became significant. Cars, computer parts, and telecommunications all were shipped to the United States from Japan to such an extent that our imports began exceeding our exports. Our major importer was becoming Japan. Additionally, our output per worker fell from 4 percent in the midfifties to 0.4 percent in the late eighties.

Our workforce was becoming less and less efficient. We were making products that other countries didn't want. American products were becoming so unreliable that we were buying Japanese versions of our products.

Another significant date is 1982. Theoretically the United States woke up in 1982. We began to take the word *quality* seriously. Prior to

F I G U R E   2–1

American and Japanese Quality Outputs

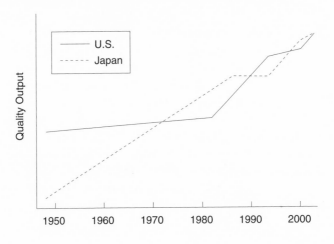

1982, the United States defined quality differently than the Japanese. Our definition was "a real good product." The Japanese, through the tutelage of W. Edwards Deming and other quality gurus, had begun defining quality as "conformance to standards." The first time I read that definition, I simply could not understand it. Quite frankly, I preferred "a real good product." The word *standards* was the key. For example, one of the standards was zero defects. That meant products with no defects—absolutely none. U.S. products had defects and we were concerned about them. We were doing the best we could with defects. Some manufacturers even measured defects and decided that 70 or 80 percent defects was doing pretty darn good. The United States was settling for imperfection; consequently, that was exactly what we got. Close enough was our philosophy.

This quality issue even began to have an impact on our service culture. Its impact was caused by customer service employees who began to think that outgoing, positive, friendly service was just too much. The Japanese believed that outgoing, positive, friendly service was nonnegotiable. It was zero defects. It was pride. It was part of their heritage. We disagreed.

Close-enough manufacturing and service resulted in a weakening of our competitive abilities, especially from a global point of view. A point in fact is the good old VCR. Sony bought it, spent a few billion dollars and 20 years refining it, and marketed it. Today, the United States does not make one VCR. Not one! The Japanese have capitalized on a short-sighted U.S. evaluation and now control a $40-billion-a-year market.

The world is changing and the United States's ability to change as rapidly as other countries lagged until the early 1990s.

The United States became intensely aware of its inability to remain globally competitive around 1988. Industry leaders began adopting a more realistic approach to developing, manufacturing, and marketing products and services. Japan began coasting. Rapidly the momentum reversed. The United States, learning from more innovative countries and cultures, internalized the scope of changes necessary to remain the dominant global supplier. This cyclical shift of power forces the key players to constantly change and improve.

It is not the issue of Japan versus the rest of the world. In fact, Japan's concept of growth is shared by South Korea, Taiwan, Singapore, and Hong Kong (the four baby dragons). The Pacific Rim accounts for a major portion of our worldwide economic growth. Additionally, countries such as Ireland and Scotland have persuaded major corporations to locate manufacturing plants in their countries and in so doing have become competitive industrial countries. Finally, the half-hearted unification of Europe in 1992 will, at some point, create a single economic power whose impact will be felt worldwide, especially with the Eastern European influence.

We have talked primarily about the changes affecting business and economy. But change is much broader. We really should look at change from a sociological point of view; in other words, how do members of one generation affect another generation?

If you are 25 and reading this book, why are your values different from mine? Is it only because I am 55? Or is it because you are impacted by the values (or lack thereof) of my generation? You are the way you are because of the way you were raised and the environment in which you were raised.

Individuals raised during the Depression developed an intense concern about security and money. My parents were both raised during that era. Money became such an important part of their lives because there was very little of it. Money was so hard to come by that people became obsessed with the lack of it. Because it affected my parent's lives, they naturally passed on those lessons to me and my brothers. Our lives, then, were guided by my parents' lessons. We were raised with an intense fear of going broke, mainly because my grandfather went broke during the Depression. It wasn't the fear of being poor. It was the fear of going broke.

A different culture would be that of the affluent young adults of the mid- to late eighties. We called them Yuppies. Their parents were in their late 50s; many were involved in either World War II or Korea. That culture is different than mine, and there is just 5 to 10 years between the parents of the Yuppies and my generation. My generation was involved in Vietnam. This is important because my children are different than Yuppies due to the values instilled in them by my wife and me and our contemporaries.

Different generations beget different attitudes. That is so because of what each generation has learned and the environment in which it was learned. Today, we live in a society characterized by many individuals who are negative. My generation taught their children how to describe things by telling what is wrong with it. We were raised learning about how corrupt our government was. We saw pictures of students being shot at Kent State. We were witnesses to the racial hypocrisy in this country. So, naturally, we were a suspicious generation. Combine that with the fact that we were a

spoiled generation: no wars per se, good economic climate, relatively comfortable existence. Spoiled and suspicious leads to a negative culture.

That is different from the almost naive optimism of the late forties
and fifties. This does not mean that *all* Americans were positive 30 years
ago. Or, for that matter, that *all* Americans are negative today. It is a general momentum like the ebb and flow of a tide. Not all of the water is
coming in when the tide comes in; actually some of the water is going out.
But we are not aware of the water going out because most of it is coming
in. We see extremes and the extremes cloud the details. Similarly, we see
and react to the extreme beliefs of our society.

Life moves forward in cycles—ups and downs; business cycles,
cycles of art, religious cycles, societal cycles. These cycles alternate from
positive to negative. Usually, a bad business cycle follows a good business cycle. From a much more subjective point of view, good cycles of
art follow bad cycles of art (or vice versa). From a societal point of view,
a positive culture springs from a negative culture (and vice versa).

The cycle that most impacted my generation's expectations and values started in the midforties and continued well into the late fifties, and
even early sixties. For argument's sake, I have chosen VJ Day (August
14, 1945) as the beginning and President John F. Kennedy's assassination
(November 23, 1963) as the ending of that particular cycle. Eighteen
years—6,671 days.

Looking at the chart in Figure 2–2, you will see five such cycles.
The first, from 1914 to 1929, was a positive cycle reflecting good times
for the United States. More people moved to the United States than to any
other country. It was the land of opportunity, reportedly free of religious
persecution and opportunistic government. The cycle started on June 28,
1914, with the assassination of Archduke Francis Ferdinand of Austria-
Hungary in Sarajevo (ironically in Bosnia-Herzegovina), the official
beginning of World War I, and lasted until 1929 when the stock market
crashed—15 years.

The cycle didn't start promptly on June 28, nor did it stop promptly
on October 29. Those dates signify events that triggered a change in
thinking. The apex of those cycles is indicated by the event at the top of
the cycle; for example, Prohibition was the apex of the first cycle.

The second cycle covers the stock market crash in 1929 to VJ Day in
1945. Sixteen years—5,764 days. This cycle's apex was the rise of Hitler
in roughly 1933. During this cycle, few immigrants came to the United
States. It was no longer the land of opportunity; people were starving.

F I G U R E   2–2

Cycles of American Cultures

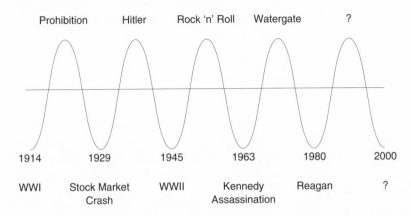

| Prohibition | Hitler | Rock 'n' Roll | Watergate | ? |

| 1914 | 1929 | 1945 | 1963 | 1980 | 2000 |

| WWI | Stock Market Crash | WWII | Kennedy Assassination | Reagan | ? |

The third cycle was my cycle: VJ Day to Kennedy's assassination. The apex was rock 'n' roll music. Historians may roll their eyes when they read of rock 'n' roll music as a major societal shift, but it solidified the age of cool with Elvis, hoodlums, and so on.

The fourth cycle went from Kennedy's assassination to the Reagan presidency. The apex was Vietnam and the Nixon years. It was 17 years of increasingly progressive disenchantment with society's institutions. It was, interestingly enough, the drug era: Timothy Leary, marijuana, speed, and cocaine. Reality seemed so uncomfortable that many Americans found they could escape into the Beatles' "Lucy in the Sky with Diamonds" and reality no longer existed.

The fifth cycle is now. What is the apex? Will it be the spawning of violence in the United States? Or will it be global—Desert Storm? Will the democratizing of Eastern Europe be the apex? If this cycle started in 1980, does that mean that 1992 was the beginning of a negative cycle?

Clearly, the economics of the American culture are dictating changes to the American people. Similarly, other countries have their own societal cycles. It is different today because the speed and depth of communications have almost made us one global society. Perhaps the future will measure only one global shift in attitudes. So, we go through a variety of cycles. Some are good and some are bad. Those who pull through the cycles are the ones who are capable of changing the way they think, not just changing the way they act.

The future shows us that our changes will be bigger because the arena is bigger: global versus domestic. The rules have changed because the dominant players have changed. The biggest task ahead of us is believing that we must change—learning how we must change and then changing.

CHANGES IN BANK BRANCHES OVER THE NEXT DECADE

There will be fewer branches in most industrialized countries over the next decade. Branches will be highly automated and service driven—not transaction oriented. There will be more ATM and debit centers. There will be fewer full-time employees in the branches. Bank branches are physically becoming part of major retail centers, such as supermarket banking; they are changing and will continue to change the way we think about banking.

Banks will continue cutting expenses and increasing sales, those two concepts are creating strong banks during the nineties. Look, for example, at the financial logic of supermarket banking: (1) A bank pays rent on 400 square feet in a supermarket rather than owning or renting a brick-and-mortar asset of 1,500 to 2,000 square feet. (2) Eighty percent of the customers who walk by a supermarket bank window are someone else's customers. (3) A supermarket customer shops 2.6 times a week versus a brick-and-mortar customer who visits their branch on average 1.3 times per month.

Sometimes we think making money involves getting complicated. Actually the best ideas are simple. As long as we keep it simple, we can contribute to the success of our individual banks.

I visited an executive of a major corporation a few months ago. On the walls of his opulent office were honorary mementoes and recognitions . . . and one strange framed statement. It said:

K I S, S

I asked him what kissing had to do with the search for profits. He laughed and wrote out on a piece of paper for me what KIS,S stands for:

Keep It Simple, Stupid

The retail areas will be carefully scrutinized over the next decade because banking is highly vulnerable to both excessive expenses and lagging sales. That doesn't mean you will be firing half your staff. It doesn't mean that you must trick customers into doing more business with you. It means that part of your job will be to sensitize yourself to expenses and income—downsizing will be a logical process in your branch. The successful branch manager of the twenty-first century will be highly skilled in using behavioral management techniques, being entrepreneurial, and performing additional responsibilities.

CHANGE–AN UNNATURAL PHENOMENON

So you will change. You may not want to. You might be fairly comfortable right now, and change might be something you fight. You will either change or your bank will find someone else to run your branch who is fully in tune with the nineties. That could be the bad news.

How do you change?

I remember when I quit smoking almost daily for six months—every morning I'd start again. I wanted to quit. I watched my five-pack-a-day father-in-law die of cancer. My fingers had that disgusting yellow hue. Many of my pants had tiny little burn holes in the lap. I'm told my breath was offensive. One afternoon I quit. After dinner I was a raging idiot, irritable and abrupt. So I went to bed early. The next morning I felt proud. I thought about a cigarette from the time I woke up until 10. Only until 10 because at 10 I gave in and lit one!

I wanted to change but couldn't. Why not? Because I was obsessed with the cigarette. Quitting smoking is a short-range change. It simply required me to change the way I acted. Short range—I didn't believe it. I just quit. I thought about my next cigarette and that blissful high. Oh to be a little dizzy again.

You either change the way you act (short-term change) or you change the way you think (long-term change). You might say, "Sure do need to change. Got to reorganize my branch. Spend more time out of the branch calling on businesses. Yep, got to do those things."

But you don't. You don't because you don't think differently about your role as a branch manager. You might go so far as to have weekly sales meetings with your people. And you might do it for four or five weeks. Then they sputter out. You get too busy. You have to drop something. Can't burn the candle at both ends, you might think. So you quit the sales meeting thing since no one seems to care anyway.

You have to figure out how a branch manager of the nineties thinks. Then you have to think that way. You have to give yourself time, and you have to have periodic measurement processes. Remember the definition of quality? Conformance to standards. Looked at another way, that means setting realistic goals or standards that are quantitative and conforming to those goals. It is the adherence to those goals and the constant focus on meeting those goals that makes you begin to think like a branch manager of the nineties.

Change the way you think and you will effect long-term change. Change the way you act and you will only change temporarily. Here is a formula for change:

$$C = (D + V + S) > X$$

C is change. Change equals the sum of D, dissatisfaction; V, a realistic vision of what you are changing to; and S, the first step in that change. Those three items have to be greater than X (the pain of making the change) or you won't change.

Clearly, these elements of the formula need clarification.

D–Dissatisfaction If you are fully satisfied with your progress in your business life and if management's constant pushing for increased productivity does not bother you, you probably won't change. You are not dissatisfied, the first element in our change formula. If you are proud of yourself and believe your branch is doing everything possible to become a branch of the nineties, you won't change. One must seek change to make the change.

Branch managers that I know are generally dissatisfied. They complain to me that they are not making enough money, that senior management doesn't know what they're talking about, that they're juggling so many balls they're going to drop one soon, that no one appreciates what they do, that they are in dead-end jobs, and on and on. The really good branch managers are dissatisfied; so are many of the very bad ones.

V–A Realistic Vision The second element of the formula is difficult because the word *realistic* is the key part. You could visualize yourself happily calling on small companies, bringing in large deposits, and making large loans. However, after that visualizing process, you might chuckle and snort, "Nonsense. It's not realistic."

What is a realistic vision? What is the change in your thinking versus the change in your actions? Perhaps it is the admission that you are spending too much time on operational tasks. Perhaps you need to see yourself delegating responsibilities and having it *not* work out exactly the way you hoped for. You must see yourself realistically. Whatever you do is not going to work exactly the way you planned. That is realism. So see yourself *making* it work. See yourself struggling to adopt a new management style. Then see yourself happy in the role of external selling, happy in the role of an internal sales manager.

The vision must be worked on. If you are dissatisfied enough, you will begin to put this concept of a realistic vision into focus. Utter dissatisfaction will result in a more defined vision. The vision will not be totally accurate the first time. Few are. So you will mentally visualize, modify, and visualize again. The more you modify, the more the dissatisfaction makes the vision an honest one.

So, if I might invent a word, you *dissatisfize* to visualize.

S—The First Step   What is the first step in becoming a branch manager of the nineties? Is it racing to your car and calling on every community business within a five-mile radius of your branch? Is it badgering your CSRs to improve sales? Is it not hiring that teller you know you need? What is it? If it were quitting smoking, would the first step be to stop smoking? Or would it be to consciously observe nonsmokers and to look for the positive health benefits?

So, as a branch manager, you must find the real first step. It varies depending on the individual. It could be sales, it could be downsizing, it could be time management, it could be more conceptual. Most often, the first step is education. You must learn before you can do.

You must learn by seeking education, and you must provide education. Develop a series of 20-minute staff meetings to inform your staff about the changes that are happening in banking today and will happen in the future.

Meeting 1

I. Introduction
    A. Introduce the concept of these four weekly meetings.
        1. Preparing ourselves for change.
        2. Creating open communication to facilitate change.
    B. Change from what to what.

II. Content
   A. How your employees' jobs will change (grow or disappear) over the next five years.
      1. Use excerpts from Chapters 3 and 4.
         a. Societal cycles, and so on.

Meeting 2
II. Content (continued)
   B. How your branch is organized now and how it will be organized in the future (an extension of IB).
      1. Begin talking about a sales culture. It is the driving force of this change.
      2. Discuss operational versus sales tasks.

Meeting 3
II. Content (continued)
   C. Internal selling versus external selling (Chapter 11).
      1. Introduce the concept of regularly scheduled sales meetings within the branch.
         a. Who attends?
         b. Who is in charge?
         c. Set specific dates.

Meeting 4
II. Content (continued)
   D. Measuring sales performance (page 154).

$$C = (D + V + S) > X$$

Change equals the sum of D, dissatisfaction; V, a realistic vision of what they are changing to; and S, the first step in that change. Those three items have to be greater than X (the pain of making the change) or your staff won't change.

It is really the interrelationship of D and V that creates the ongoing need for change.

SUMMARY

1. America has progressed from being comfortable as a domestic economy to being threatened by the prospect of becoming part of a global economy.

2. Financial institutions will undergo many changes during the next decade. They will be more automated. There will be fewer employees in the branches. In many countries, there will be fewer branches. Banks will be cutting expenses and increasing sales.

3. The following is the formula for change. $C = (D + V + S) > X$, where C is change. Change equals the sum of D, dissatisfaction; V, a realistic vision of what you are changing to; and S, the first step in that change. Those three items have to be greater than X (the pain of making the change) or you won't change.

CHAPTER 3

Selling Strictly Defined

Selling in banking is an important part of the changing process, perhaps the single most important part of a bank's ability to remain competitive. Yet this issue—selling—is resisted at a puzzlingly high rate.

I once talked to a friend of mine, and in the process of our conversation I politely asked him how his son was doing.

"Not real well," he answered dejectedly.

"Sorry to hear that," I replied, politely. "Didn't he graduate from Cornell?"

"Yeah. Majored in electrical engineering. Really bright kid. What a shame."

"What happened?"

"He became a salesman."

"A salesman," I repeated.

"Yeah, poor kid. Probably couldn't do any better."

For years and even today, the image of the salesperson has been negative. The major hurdle in developing a sales culture within an organization is to refocus employees' thinking regarding the word *selling*.

I used to work for a major Fortune 500 company back in the early sixties. They had a staff of several hundred salespeople throughout the world, all carrying embossed business cards listing their names and their job: Sales Representative, these cards read. Someone in management decided that the company could increase sales if their people had different titles, so new cards were printed and shipped to all of the sales representatives. The new cards listed their job as Marketing Representative. Of course, it was the same job. They just put a different label on it. Think of the message this sent out to the sales force. The job is the same; the title is different because the perception of sales—even by salespeople—is negative. Many bright, discerning business minds in college today are choosing professions unsuited to them to avoid being salespersons.

At the start of my sales seminars for bankers, I ask the class to make a list of adjectives that best describe a salesperson. Over a period of years, I have pulled together this "banker's dozen":

Sleazy, dishonest, manipulative, insincere,
shifty, pushy, untrustworthy, opportunistic,
overbearing, fast-talking, evasive, intimidating.

I have memorized these words and can say them very quickly. Anytime anyone in my seminars (or anywhere) says something stereotypical about salespeople, I rattle off the banker's dozen.

"Exactly," I quite often hear. I shake my head and think, pity.

If our society thinks the profession of selling is best described by the banker's dozen, then it would naturally denigrate the overall profession of selling. A truly effective salesperson is able to describe a product or service to someone in a way that allows that person to see how the product or service will satisfy his needs.

Selling is a process of needs satisfaction. A good salesperson learns what the prospect's needs are and then systematically matches those needs to the benefits of the salesperson's product. The sales process balances (1) the needs of the customer with (2) the benefits of the product. Really simple stuff!

Problems occur when a salesperson promises benefits that the product does not offer or preys on the customer's emotions to the point that false needs are created. "Aha," you say. "Exactly what salespeople do."

Sleazy, dishonest, manipulative, insincere,
shifty, pushy, untrustworthy, opportunistic,
overbearing, fast-talking, evasive, intimidating.

If the need for the product doesn't exist, the sale should not happen. When the salesperson creates a false need through emotions, she is doing an injustice to the customer.

A good example is some of our more illustrious television ministries; for example, Jimmy Swaggert and Jim Bakker preyed on their customers' emotions, offering spiritual benefits.

When a salesperson puts personal gain ahead of the customer, it is easy to take advantage of the customer. That dilemma goes far beyond the traditional definitions of sales into medicine.

A major issue in the field of clinical psychology today is determining when the psychologist quits helping the patient and begins taking advantage of the patient. How long is that relationship supposed to last? In an attempt to assure income, do psychologists ever prolong the therapy for cash flow?

Psychology is very close to sales. Here the salesperson (the psychologist) is satisfying the needs of the customer (the patient) by blending the psychologist's knowledge of the illness with the patient's need for the cure. The product? Knowledge.

Psychologists aren't the only professionals who sell their services. Not too long ago I visited my dentist. He cleaned my teeth as he usually does and warned me that I needed to floss more or my gums would fall out. Then he produced one of those 8-inch-diameter mirrors. He held it about a foot in front of my mouth.

"Look at the front tooth, Dwight," he said shaking his head.

I rolled back my lips in an insincere smile and looked. "Yep, those are mine," I said sarcastically.

"Look at the size of one of your centrals versus the other."

"My whats?"

"Your centrals. Your two upper front teeth."

"Yeah. What about them?"

"See how big one is compared to the other?"

"That's cause one is false."

"Yes. This one," he said, tapping on one of my front teeth.

"Yep."

"It looks a bit lopsided, Dwight. I mean it's longer and wider than the other one."

"You think it looks funny?"

"Not funny," he hedged. "Maybe peculiar. It is noticeable. You're constantly in front of people making presentations aren't you?"

"Yeah."

"And because of your business, you must have your picture on your books and brochures. Don't you?"

"Uh-huh," I mumbled. "I never looked at it that way." I rolled back my lips again. "It is kinda weird."

"How long have you had that false tooth?"

"Oh, I dunno. Since I was. . . let's see. It was knocked out when I was around 10. Then I had it replaced a number of times. Not since I was 19. Nineteen," I replied.

"And you're 56."

"Fifty-five," I corrected.

"You've had that false tooth for 35 years?"

"A hell of a bargain, uh?"

"I'll say. But false teeth and real teeth wear differently. Because of chewing habits, or whatever, your front teeth have been worn down. But this false tooth hasn't," he said, tapping on the tooth. "That's why it looks so big."

"Huh," I said holding the mirror and looking at my teeth.

"Looks a little peculiar."

"I don't remember it being that obvious."

"Probably wasn't, but over the years your other central got worn down and this fella just stayed the same size." He tapped again.

"I never realized that before."

"Yep. Looks pretty obvious."

"Sure does. What's this gonna cost?"

"I think we can do it for $700. Heck, while I'm in there I'll fill in the unsightly gap between your two centrals."

Consider the sales process my dentist went through. He talked about my needing to look better. He spelled out the disadvantages of not having his product. He countered my objections and finally he stated the price in a way that allowed me to feel I was getting a bargain.

My dentist is a salesperson. If I were to tell him that, he would feel insulted. He sees himself as a professional dentist. A salesman is lower in status from his point of view, that is, sleazy, dishonest, manipulative, insincere, shifty, pushy, untrustworthy, opportunistic, overbearing, fast-talking, evasive, and intimidating.

Everyone is selling something. Ministers are salespeople; they are selling ideas. You are buying their ideas. Otherwise there would be no collection plate. Doctors are salespeople. You approach them with a problem. They ask questions and satisfy your needs for a fee. But doctors are called doctors. Ministers are called ministers. Sadly, in *Death of a*

Salesman Willy Loman was called a salesman and the entire profession has been paying for that for years!

The kind of selling that Willy Loman did, and the image that most people have of selling, is that of the pushy, aggressive, hard seller. Because of that image, people don't consider doctors or ministers as salespeople. Selling is, however, a fairly broad profession. Just like other professions, selling has a lot of versions to it.

Stated simply, there is soft selling and there is hard selling. Soft selling is what my dentist does. Hard selling is that horrible thing that most people associate with sales. There are variations of hard selling. The door-to-door vacuum cleaner salesperson. The used car salesperson. Probably a bit more current would be the sales process involved in selling time-share condominiums. I receive a letter in the mail, promising a gift. I pursue the gift while the promisor of the gift pursues me for a condo. They call me. They challenge me. They might even suggest, "You can't really afford something like this. Can you, Mr. Ritter?" They will take a conditional down payment . . . just to hold a unit. The down payment is refundable. Have you ever tried to get it back?

When you walk into a new car showroom, the first thing the salesperson asks is, "Are you here to buy, or are you just looking?" If you are just looking, they will leave you alone. If you are there to buy, they'll be on you like a wet T-shirt! The hard sell focuses on a time-to-buy format, probing to find out when you plan on buying. "Is this something you could do today?" they might ask. Hard-sell salespersons don't really care about satisfying your needs. They spend more time closing the sale rather than listening. They use the element of time as a weapon, constantly forcing you to make decisions because of time constraints.

Note the varying degrees of intensity spread out over a fairly academic sales process in Figure 3–1. Here we illustrate the major differences between hard selling and soft selling. As you can see, the two styles of selling are at extreme opposites when it comes to needs fulfillment and closing.

THE SALES PROCESS

Because soft selling relies on knowing the customer, the presales planning stage of the model requires a soft seller to concentrate heavily in this area. The most heavily concentrated part would be the needs fulfillment stage. To fulfill a customer's needs, you have to know quite a bit about

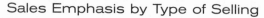

F I G U R E   3–1

Sales Emphasis by Type of Selling

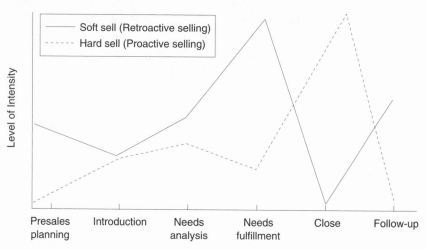

the customer. If you don't care about the customer's needs, you begin caring too much about the success or failure of the sale.

Presales Planning

Sales starts with getting oneself prepared to sell, for example, having brochures, files, and so on. Also it includes researching customers, developing call lists, and culling those lists.

Introduction

Once you have the presales material carefully sorted, you're ready to meet the customer. Depending on the kind of selling you do, meeting the customer can vary from a casual meeting at a chamber of commerce function to a structured meeting at your desk to a formal meeting with a businessperson in his office.

Needs Analysis

What are your customer's needs in relation to your product or service? That is often different than what your customer thinks she needs. As we call on businesses, we have to determine what are the financial needs of each prospect. What are their financial and business goals? Where can the bank get involved? Financial needs can run the gamut from needing a better cash flow, improved sales, controlling expenses, accounting assistance, or even someone to talk to.

Needs Fulfillment

Bankers fulfill financial needs with the right kind of products or services. Matching our services with the appropriate financial needs means learning how businesses make money.

Close

Letting the prospective customer know that your bank can satisfy those needs leads to asking for the order, picking a time to begin the business relationship, outlining the costs of the service, and saying in effect, "Let's get started."

There are many theories on closing the sale: trial closing, assumptive closing, two-for-one closing, and fix one, close two. Many industries focus on this part of the sales cycle. Banking, however, should be so needs-based that closing becomes a natural part of needs fulfillment.

Follow-up

Follow up on any unsettled issues most often by phone; sometimes by letter, in person, or both. The follow-up must be regarded as an integral part of the sales process, especially for the banker.

Now, let's look at Figure 3–1 again. Notice how hard selling relies on defining the time frame; that is, when the sale starts and when it finishes. Time is the key, so closing the sale for an automobile salesperson is where his energy should be focused. From the time you walk into an automobile showroom until you leave, the salesperson concentrates on closing the sale. All of the salesperson's energy is directed at determining when you will buy.

For persons involved in more aggressive sales, the preplanning phase is of little interest. They don't need files on their customers. They don't need to analyze thoroughly their customers' needs prior to meeting them. All they need to do is concentrate on the product.

A more sensitive selling mode requires concentrating on the customers. *The customers' needs drive the selection of the most appropriate products.*

The hard sell focuses on the product.
The soft sell focuses on the customer.

The depth of understanding of the product mix in soft selling is much more complex. You simply can't get away with schlepping financial products. Your customer knows better.

Here's a good analogy. You walk into an unscrupulous psychologist's office. She says, "What would you like to be treated for?"

"Well," you ponder. "How about depression?"

"Sorry," the psychologist says. "I don't do depression. But I have a great treatment for alcohol abuse."

"But I don't have a problem with alcohol."

"Come on," the psychologist challenges. "Everyone's got a problem with alcohol. You do drink, don't you?"

"Well, socially."

"There you go," the psychologist beams. "The first stage of treatment is to admit you have a problem!"

"But I didn't admit I had a problem. Only that I drink socially."

"That's all it takes. Just one drink."

In this example, the psychologist was focusing on the product, not on the need. She never asked what was bothering the patient. She had a product in mind. Product focusing quite often leads to high-risk selling, not necessarily hard selling. High-risk selling is rattling off a list of products at your customer or saying, "We do have a lot of other products. Are there any of them that you would be interested in?" High-risk selling invites a no.

As a branch manager, you must know the difference between hard selling and soft selling for two reasons. First, you must cultivate your own soft-selling style and, second, you must manage the in-house efforts of your platform sales team. Understanding that difference and being able to discuss it with your staff will enhance your successful sales efforts.

SUMMARY

1. For years, the image of the salesperson has been negative. The major hurdle in developing a sales culture within an organization is to reorient employees' thinking regarding the word *selling*.

2. A really great salesperson is able to describe a product or service to someone in a way that allows that person to see how the product or service will satisfy his needs.

3. Selling is a process of needs satisfaction. A salesperson learns what her prospect's needs are. Then those needs are systematically matched to the benefits of the salesperson's product.

4. Stated simply, there is hard selling and there is soft selling. Hard selling is that horrible thing that most people associate with sales. Soft selling is what my dentist and my minister do.

5. The steps in an effective sales model are as follows:
   a. Presales planning
   b. Introduction
   c. Needs analysis
   d. Needs fulfillment
   e. Close
   f. Follow up

6. The hard sell focuses on the product. The soft sell focuses on the customer.

CHAPTER 4

Identifying the Small Business Customer

Branch managers worldwide face the same issue: Where do I find good business customers? How do I go about meeting them?

Should your employer send you into a new community as a new branch manager for a major national or regional bank, what do you do? You don't know your employees. You don't know your neighborhood. You wait for the bank to send you a list of businesses in your community, but they don't. Somewhere in college you read that you should join the local Rotary. Besides, your branch is chaotic. The last branch manager left you an organizational can of worms: not enough help in the branch, lines running out the door, and a major morale problem.

At the most recent regional meeting, the regional coordinator talked about the importance of calling on the local business community. The real issue is whether the bank enforces the officer call program. I have spent years reading officer call sheets; many were very amusing. Month after month, I am expected to believe that a particular branch manager is calling on the local Dunkin' Donuts. What happens is that branch manager writes down Dunkin' Donuts once just to see if he can get away with it. If it works, he will write it down again and again. On the other side, the branch administrators are stuck with the duty of managing the officer call program. All they really are responsible for is checking to be sure that the managers make a certain number of calls each month. Can you see what's happening? That means all the officer has to do is report names of businesses. He doesn't have to do any business with them, just report their names. I know managers around the world who put their dentists' names down and the local restaurants that they frequent. It worked in the past.

Now in all fairness to branch managers, officer call programs were invented by people who don't know anything about selling; but they do know about numbers. People who don't understand selling tend to simplify it. They think selling is calling on people, as in "Call on enough people and someone will buy." Ever hear that one before? Well it's true except you get so many rejections that you begin to doubt your product and your own ability as a businessperson.

The truth of the matter is that you should know who to call on first. Don't "smokestack" if you are a banker. Now let me clarify what smokestacking is. It is driving down the street and randomly choosing any business and walking in without an appointment or any knowledge of the business at all; no advance letter, no phone call, no prior knowledge of the business or the industry. Just walk in—cold.

Many bankers brag about their success. I shake my head in pity. They certainly must not have any idea of their relative dollar value. Take, for example, their hourly rate. A branch manager who makes 20 smokestacks might get a solid customer once. That means this person was driving around the countryside, knocking on doors, and being rejected 19 times. Assume he spent 45 minutes per smokestack, on the average; that includes driving to the stack and back, and the eventual rejection. So what is a manager's hourly rate—$14.00 per hour? He has just spent 14.25 hours (19 calls) being rejected. That comes to $199.50. That doesn't include the automotive expenses and the related lunches. It might be easier for a smokestack to ask for around $250 to burn each month!

What about the one account? Is it worth the $250? It's not just $250. It is the expense of $250 per month. It is cumulative because it is a recurring expense.

Once you know about a specific business and you have done your homework and know the principals, read up on the industry, sent an advance letter, and called for an appointment, your odds increase. You will spend less time getting turned down. You will hear the word *no* less. Most important, you will be a more productive salesperson because your sales-rejection expense will go down and your success ratio will go up.

How do you know whom to call on? Randomly pick names from the phone book? Arrive in a new town and reach for the phone book, then send out letters and call? Actually, those odds are better than smoke-stacking. There is, however, a better way.

Let's examine this issue in great detail in a way that would cover the new branch manager in Scottsburg, Indiana; the new managing director in Zurich, Switzerland; or the new assistant manager in Enniskillen, Ireland. This is a big issue because if you don't understand the workings of your business community, you cannot be an active part of your bank's external sales program.

MARKET ANALYSIS

You must learn how to do an honest market analysis. This is not a huge, bound volume with a statistical analysis and area trends. No, this is your own market analysis. Based on your unique style, it is an active market analysis because you developed it and therefore must use it. If it is a 400-page commissioned product, you won't read it, and even if you do, you won't know what it means. So, therefore, you won't use it.

As a branch banker (or area banker), you need to identify your most profitable prospects. When I entered the international consulting business, I used to plan calls in Dublin, Amsterdam, Barcelona, Zurich, and Curacao. I planned from Boston! I wasted more money on the phone and traveling to prospects in countries who had no intention of using my services. But they loved the idea of having a Boston consultant calling on them. My sales costs were so high that my first piece of international business was an absolute loss from a dollars-and-cents point of view. I couldn't possibly have charged what I should have to partially recoup my costs of getting that first piece of business. Thank God I owned the business! Anyone else would have fired me for imprudent business practices.

Not a smart salesman, I was unaware of what profitable prospects were. I had heard: "New business is everyone's business." "All prospects are prospects." "A sale is a sale is a sale." In fact, that is not true. Selling is not asking every single person you meet for business hoping that one might say yes. As a banker, you are looking for more than sales. You are looking for profits. That means good loans, solid deposits, low sales expenses, low transaction costs, and profits.

To do an individualized market analysis, get out a local map and pinpoint your branch. Then draw a circle that might encompass a five-mile radius. Make sure that radius does not overlap another branch of your bank. If it does, you might want to shorten the radius or share your market analysis with the other branch. Regardless, you need to define your territory. Pick one just the right size for you.

The first step would be to reach for your local Yellow Pages. Open it to Chambers of Commerce. There you will find the local chamber. You might also want to look under Associations. There you will find a number of organizations that will be very specific to particular industries.

You will need some broader, more general organizations such as a chamber of commerce to get yourself plugged into your community. Chambers are also sources for other community organizations. So, if you asked me where to start, I would tell you to pick a chamber.

Now go to your local chamber of commerce or community service organization and join it. Sit down with someone there and show her your map. Tell her you want to find the names of the businesses in your market area. This in itself is a sales job. You need to make that association person feel important and special. Spend some time learning about the organization. Learn who the principals are. Who is on the board of directors? What are the specialty committees? This helps you learn about the community.

Most chambers publish a membership directory and members are entitled to a copy. Spend some time browsing through the directory to learn who in the directory is in your market. Is there someone at the chamber who can tell you about some of the businesses in your area? Who are the owners, the management? Gather names, personal facts, other associations you might want to join. Be supportive and positive and, above all, grateful.

Now make a competition diagram as shown in Figure 4–1. Your competition list must include those banks within a radius of twice your own market radius. Why twice the size of your market radius? Because your competition, if it has been around for a while, has evolved out of its market area. Or it might be that your competition is pursuing a larger area in which to call. So just to be on the safe side, make its radius twice yours.

Make a list of the banks and their addresses, then drive around your market. Look at your competition's branches. If they don't know you, go into their branches. Pick up some brochures. You should be able to tell, just by looking at a branch, whether they are 100 percent consumer-oriented and whether they take this officer call thing seriously. Many small thrifts make only token efforts at business development. Consequently, they are not factors in the market. That is not a universal comment, how-

F I G U R E   4–1

A Competition Diagram

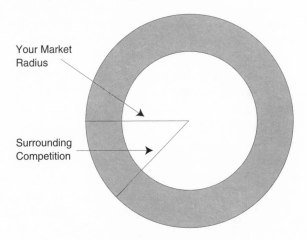

Your Market
Radius

Surrounding
Competition

ever, because other thrifts have become major forces in the small- to medium-sized business market. But you can tell. Look around. Look at the branch manager. How many CSRs are there? Does it look staffed well enough to send the branch manager out into the field? Take notes.

So now you know your competition. Your local chamber has provided you with a list of businesses. If you did a thorough job with the chamber personnel, they have given some names of good businesspeople, businesses that have been around for a while. These are the strong, well-managed, steady-growth business that you are looking for.

Send a preapproach letter to each strong, well-managed business. Chapter 7 includes sample preapproach letters and a rationale for using them.

POWER STRUCTURES–THE ENLIGHTENED SELF-INTEREST

In every town or city, there exists a power structure. It is not fictitious. A power structure is made up of several of the community's leading citizens. It is not composed of members of appointed offices. It is simply composed of several concerned citizens who meet on a regular basis for the betterment of the community. Now many of you are saying,

"Baloney! Who does he think he's kidding! Town leaders are not interested in the betterment of the community. They are interested in the betterment of their pockets!"

I ask you to rethink your position here because thriving communities are literally run by selfless power structures. I say selfless with a
slight degree of hesitation because there is an element of personal ego
gratification involved. But if these business leaders want to stay promi-
nent in their community and reap the personal rewards inherent in a growing community, they must develop such a seemingly selfless perspective
for the survival of the community.

Power structures concern themselves with racial and sexual inequal-
ities, corrupt governments, local education issues, land development
issues—almost anything that impacts a community in a major way. Power
structures are staffed by concerned citizens on a volunteer basis.
Regularly, these groups meet informally for lunch or dinner and literally
cut across all political bounds. If they are real workable power structures,
they wield more power than political establishments.

Keep in mind, a power structure receives no publicity because in all
reality members of successful power structures don't even want people to
know they exist. Over time, though, a community knows who comprises
its power structure and they are quietly well known.

The thing that holds power structures together is enlightened self-
interest. All who are part of this elite group have their own enlightened
self-interests and these interests become checks and balances on the
direction the group is moving.

In Boston (my town), there is a power structure. It is known as The
Vault in local newspapers. The political cartoonists politely acknowledge
its existence. The members are a small group of highly successful
bankers, lawyers, and insurance executives. And in a town the size of
Boston—with the Kennedy family, Harvard, an ex-governor who ran for
president (Dukakis), and another one who might (William Weld)—The
Vault can literally cut through the system.

As a member of your business community, you should know who is
part of your power structure. It is most often a powerful banker, a lawyer,
and frequently, the newspaper editor as well as a large family business head.

You might have to ask. Don't be embarrassed. Savvy chamber personnel will know what you are talking about. You are not asking because
you want to be a member since membership doesn't formally exist. You

F I G U R E   4–2

The Power Structure in _____

Name	Profession	Company

want to know who runs the town and who their friends are. Which organizations do they belong to? As you are identifying your community's power structure, fill in the grid in Figure 4–2.

Any new major financing will certainly be on the power structure's agenda. If a major corporation is moving to town, they will know about it. Many issues will not be relevant to you strictly as a banker but as a citizen. Many of these nonconnected issues could become business opportunities further on down the line.

Success in your community as a banker means you must know the political climate—who's in charge, the power structure, and who's making money and who isn't. As you begin to get a feel for your community, your level of comfort for confidently calling on companies will increase and your success will also increase.

Don't be naive and think that there isn't a power structure or be so opinionated that you think all power structures are bad. Power structures have proven to be positive, while the politicians or single struggling businesses tend to be corrupt.

S U M M A R Y

1. Don't smokestack if you are a banker. Smokestacking is randomly driving down the street, seeing a business (any business), and walking in without an appointment or any knowledge of the business at all: no advance letter, no phone call, no prior knowledge of the business or industry.
2. Bankers should know who are their most profitable prospects.
3. The first step to reach your market is to use your local Yellow Pages. Open it to Chambers of Commerce. There you will find

the local chamber. You might also want to look under Associations. There you will find a number of organizations that will be very specific to particular industries.

4. Chambers publish a membership directory and members are entitled to a copy. Spend some time browsing through the directory to determine what your business market is.

5. Be familiar with every bank in your marketing area.

6. A power structure is made up of several of the community's leading citizens. It is not composed of members appointed to office. It is simply composed of several concerned citizens who meet on a regular basis for the betterment of the community.

CHAPTER 5

Improving Sales Communications

What is selling from a behavioral point of view?

Selling is primarily communicating with other humans—*with* is the key. *Communicating with* means *talking to* and *listening to*. Psychologists talk with their patients. Priests, ministers, and rabbis talk with their congregations. Bankers talk with their customers. That means that we must do a lot of listening, more listening than talking, if we are any good at what we do. Salespeople listen 85 percent of the time and talk 15 percent of the time. Good salespeople, whether they are doing hard or soft sales, must be good listeners.

A good friend, who is a psychotherapist, told me he listens 100 percent of the time and talks 10 percent. His math isn't quite as good as mine, but the point is well taken. If we are going to learn about communicating with other humans, then we are going to learn a lot about listening. Even when you are talking, you are listening. You listen to yourself talk and decide if your delivery is appropriate. By watching the person you are talking to, you are, in essence, listening to his body language. Maybe, then, we do listen 100 percent and talk 10 percent.

You listen with more than your ears. Your ears allow you to hear, not to listen. Your eyes allow you to listen. They tell you how someone is dressed or physically acts. As you hear or look at something, your mind internalizes the happening. That means your mind associates what it sees and hears with something else that appears to relate to it. We call that associative process of the mind internalizing. Many people do not internalize readily. Nothing appears related to anything in the minds of many healthy people. In the "not-so-healthy" category, an obvious example would be the character in *Rain Man* played by Dustin Hoffman. An autistic savant does not internalize. For most of us, however, internalizing makes the difference between hearing and listening. We listen with all of our senses.

The three elements to communicating are body language, tone, and words. All three total 100 percent. Of the three elements, body language is the most important. It accounts for 55 percent of the total!

Body language is how someone sits. How he stands or walks. His hand movements, gestures, and posture. The way she dresses and her hairstyles. It's like watching a movie without any sound. Just watch the characters. After a while, you begin to form opinions about the characters based entirely on their body language. One's body language sends so many messages that all together one can learn a lot by just watching and internalizing.

How we say the words used in our communications process is also very important. We call it tone. How does your voice sound when you say things: whiny, gruff, melodic, precise, monotonous? Do you whistle, sigh, grunt, stammer? Take the simple, "I enjoyed meeting with you." It can come out sounding absolutely dripping with desire or cold and precise, even cynical and insincere, depending on the tone and rate of delivery. This part of the communications process accounts for 23 percent of total communications. So that leaves the words—what we say—accounting for 22 percent. The actual words account for 22 percent; the actual words are the least significant part of communicating.

Thus, it isn't so much what you say as it is how you say it and how you appear when you are saying it.

Each communication has (1) a communications sender and (2) a communications receiver. Theoretically, one person talks and the other person listens, but there is more to it than that. Nonverbal communication is very important. It is how you, as communications sender, appear in the eyes of the communications receiver. It is how you appear to listen.

You are the sum of your communications elements as you talk and as you listen. The best salespeople are the best listeners. They listen with their eyes, nodding their heads, giving positive gestures. In Figure 5–1, we summarize the elements of communication.

F I G U R E   5–1

Communications Elements

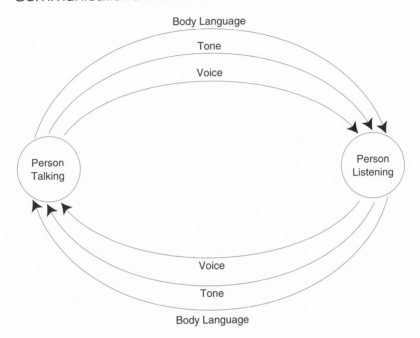

TRUST AND COMFORT

At one point in my life, I became a clinical psychologist. I felt deeply committed to understanding and helping those individuals who were confused, unhappy, and nervous. Soon I discovered that I was one of those individuals—confused, unhappy, and nervous. As a matter of fact, most people are confused, unhappy, and nervous. Confusion creates negative stress. Negative stress creates unhappiness. Our business world is made up of individuals deemed to be successful when they are promoted and make money. Consequently, when they are not promoted and do not make money, they became unhappy. When they are unhappy, they become distressed; and with distress comes nervousness.

I decided that I was pretty much like other people, and I needed to concentrate on my own development rather than getting caught up in other people's problems. However, I did learn a lot about behavior, about how to talk to people in a confined situation, and how to ask the kinds of questions that people want to answer.

One of the key concepts in working with patients as a psychotherapist is trust and comfort. Success as a psychotherapist depends, to a large degree, on having the ability to instill trust and comfort quickly. When a patient visits for the first time, the therapist has roughly 50 minutes to instill trust and comfort. The patient must trust the therapist and feel comfortable or she won't come back. If patients don't return for subsequent visits, the therapist will not be in business very long. So, a successful psychotherapist creates a high level of trust and comfort quickly and then maintains it throughout the recovery process.

That was fascinating stuff for me! I thought, If people like me, they stay. If they don't like me, they never come back. That's a scary business. You see, it doesn't make any difference whether you like them or not. Your job is to focus on the patient, not to like them.

There is virtually no difference between a good psychotherapist's basic duties and a good salesperson's basic duties. Let me clarify that so I can become more accurate. My reference to a good salesperson means a person who makes good soft sales. Remember Chapter 3, where we defined hard sales versus soft sales? Soft sales is long term; it is cultivating relationships with customers. It is finding out what their true needs are to satisfy those specific needs with specific products.

Think of two gears that power a source when interlocked. One gear is the needs of the customer. The other gear is the products of the salesperson. The source is a successful sale, as shown in Figure 5–2.

On the left are the thoughts of a customer. They create needs. The needs gear spins. If the needs are not satisfied, they will create frustration, negative stress. The soft sales process simply pushes the two gears together so that the needs gear meshes with the products gear and drives satisfaction.

The sales process must link the needs with the product or service and engage the gears. Many sales encounters are unsuccessful because the salesperson is not concerned with the customer's needs. The customer, in effect, becomes frustrated because the salesperson is focusing on the product rather than the customer's needs. The customer feels pushed.

Figure 5–2 actually illustrates a sales concept known as needs-based selling in which the salesperson bases his products on the specific needs of the customer.

F I G U R E   5–2

A Successful Soft Sale

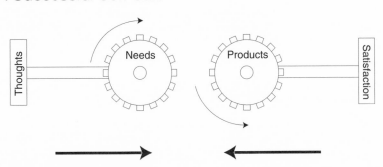

WIN-WIN SELLING

Quite frankly, I have a problem with the concept of *winning* in a sales environment. My gut feeling is that if one person wins, another person loses. That bothers me. I'm not going to sell if that is what I have to do. In reality, only unethical selling results in someone losing. What we should be looking for is a win-win sales situation. The customer buys a product and is happy. The salesperson sells a product and is happy. That doesn't bother me at all. It bothers me when someone suggests selling is pitting your manipulative abilities against your customer's. That's wrong. That's where the win-lose concept of sports and selling breaks down.

Competition should only be between you and the other salesperson; that is, the one who will get the order if you don't. The customer is an ally. Your ability to bring the customer to your side allows you to win the sale from the other salesperson.

There is a lose-win sales situation involving a salesperson and a customer, where the customer loses and the salesperson wins. Much high-pressure selling is based on this concept. The salesperson tricks the customer into buying. The customer either buys a product she doesn't need or pays too much for a product she does need. That is called lose-win. In both win-win and lose-win, a sale is made.

Much of the media treatment of the profession of selling capitalizes on the lose-win concept, for example, *Death of a Salesman* or more recently *The Tin Man.* That is why parents didn't want their children to be salespersons.

Sleazy, dishonest, manipulative, insincerely, shifty, pushy, untrustworthy, opportunistic, overbearing, fast-talking, evasive, intimidating.

As shown in Figure 5–3, there are also lose-lose situations where both the customer and the salesperson lose. No sale! The customer does not have his needs met and the salesperson does not sell her product.

When you sell financial services, you must be part of a win-win sales situation. Your CSRs have an obligation to their customers. You have an obligation to your customers.

Recently, I was working with a bank in Europe. Although it was very proud of its culture, I was distturbed from the beginning. Too many people who were telling me sales war stories were telling me about how they had tricked the customers into accepting products. They would follow up their story with a smile and knowing wink. It bothered me. They were obviously proud of the sale. They obviously thought that that was what I felt would be a good sale. It bothered me. And I didn't have the courage to confront them. Further investigation revealed that their sales culture wasn't working. Why? There aren't enough tricks to impact the bottom line. On top of that, repeat business was decreasing. And, most important, the employees were beginning to view their customers in an adversarial role. Hard, trickster selling takes a toll on customer service.

Your job is to create trust and comfort. It results in win-win sales. Repeat business, respect, and enjoyment of your job are the by-products of this kind of selling.

F I G U R E   5–3

The Sales Situations

So How Do You Do This Trust and Comfort Thing?

Learn to analyze other people's behavior and then to align your behavior more closely to theirs.

TRANSACTIONAL ANALYSIS

Interpersonal communications is a field of study that incorporates this concept. It had its beginnings back in the fifties. Eric Berne pioneered the effort when he started writing papers about personality states. Actually, he called them ego states, that is, personality styles. We are familiar with styles of communication.

Many books, such as *I'm OK, You're OK,* picked up on Berne's ego states. College texts used Berne's theories as their basis. His theory of ego states was called transactional analysis. This theory is important because it will teach you how to analyze your customers better—both business and consumer—and to be more successful in your sales efforts.

Transactional analysis describes three styles of communication; One style is adultlike, the second is parentlike, and the third is childlike. Everyone exhibits these adultlike, parentlike, and childlike characteristics daily. As we move through our routine encounters with others, we change our outward behavior so that we can get what we want.

My son wants me to prepare breakfast. He asks me in a way that he thinks will get him breakfast. If his way is agreeable to me, I will prepare breakfast. If his way is not agreeable, I won't. If he really wants breakfast, he will think about how to propose his suggestion that I prepare it.

Incidentally, my son, too, has the capability of exhibiting adultlike, parentlike, and childlike behavior. And he has the capabilities of aligning his outward personality closely to mine. (Whether he elects to do that or not is another matter.)

Let's discuss the behavior styles depicted in Figure 5–4 so we can understand more about them.

Personality Styles in Transactional Analysis

Adultlike behavior is fairly formal. It is unemotional behavior that is logical and precise. Adultlike behavior does not exhibit large variations in the tone of one's voice. It is methodical, professional, and agenda-oriented behavior.

F I G U R E   5–4

Behavior Styles of Transactional Analysis

When you first call on a business, your behavior should be adultlike, not stuffy or boring, but well-organized, professional, precise, waiting to take your cue from your customer.

Adultlike behavior is the least controversial behavior. It is so defined and structured not to be offensive. It is comfortable. Not opulent or luxurious, just comfortable. Effective adultlike behavior has no negatives. Adultlike behavior is two-way communications. Two people can carry on a conversation in adultlike behavior.

Adultlike behavior can function as an acceptable behavior in transition. That means it is a good way to act with a business customer until you learn the prospect's true personality, whereupon you will modify your behavior to more closely align with that of your customer.

Parentlike behavior is quite different than adultlike. First, it is an emotional behavior, primarily anger; and, second, it is one-way communication. The person exhibiting parentlike behavior talks at the other person. Management by intimidation is parentlike. Authoritative. Dictatorial. When planned carefully, parentlike behavior can be an effective negotiating tool, such as the person who suddenly explosively storms out of a meeting because negotiations are getting nowhere.

Childlike behavior goes from one extreme to another. It can be whiny, spoiled behavior; it can also be informal and laidback behavior. In between those extremes is what almost anyone you meet would call childlike behavior. Childlike behavior can be very manipulative, in a cute sort of way.

I have a daughter who went to college in Ithaca, New York. There is a lot of snow and many steep inclines at her school. I have a truck. Let me rephrase that, I have my favorite truck. I like it so much, I named it Big Red. I call it that because it is a big red truck.

At one winter break in school, my daughter came to me to talk. She puffed out her lower lip slightly. Her hands were clasped behind her. She moved restlessly from one foot to the next and tilted her head from one side to the other.

"Daddy," she said, sounding like she used to when her doll needed fixing. "It would be so much easier if I had Big Red on campus. I just love ole Big Red. He's so super great in the snow."

I responded by tilting my head and raising my eyebrows. "Goosey," I said, using my pet name for her. "We get a lot of snow here, too. And, I need Big Red to plow the driveway." At that point I was whining.

My daughter was acting childlike. She did so because, over the years, it seemed to be the most successful behavior to use when she wanted something from me.

And I, on the other hand, have always been a sucker for childlike behavior. She knows that. The beginning of my submission was when I called her Goosey.

Two childlike humans carrying on a communication: One wants something and has set a goal for herself. The other is resisting albeit not very well. Childlike behavior is two-way communication. It is emotional, informal, volatile, mercurial, impulsive, cutesy, and laidback.

We tend to repeat successful behavior. We are like animals gravitating toward positive behavior. "If it works, do it again," our brains say. As we observe other people's behavior, our brains locate certain behaviors they can mimic to receive pleasurable feedback. So your brain guides you toward repeating that behavior; behavioral habits are based on success. Grown men revert to baby talk with their wives. The authoritative, no-compromise manager is the same way at home.

Childlike behavior works well around other childlike behavior. It is also a dominating behavior within the family structure. So if I want to schmooze that whiny daughter of mine, I give her back some of her own medicine!

Adultlike behavior is the same. The way we deal with adultlike behavior is in an adultlike way. Parentlike behavior is different. One does not mimic parentlike behavior. That starts an emotional encounter. Parentlike behavior is a behavior in a vacuum. It is one-way, generally short-term, used for effect. Parentlike behavior is most effectively handled with adultlike behavior. In family situations, we find that parentlike behavior can also be counteracted with childlike behavior, for example, crying!

So how is this information significant from a sales point of view? If you are making a first call on a business, do it in an adultlike manner. It is the least controversial behavior, the most ordered behavior. However, it does not endear you to your customer. There is no real heart in the adultlike salesperson. The heart comes when one is able to stray from one behavior to the next. To dip into childlike; be humorous and entertaining and then slide back to adultlike. That sparkle in the salesperson's eye, that sensitivity and understanding, is all under the umbrella of control—the totally flexible adultlike behavior. Use adultlike as the home base of your personalities.

Look at the swings in behavior from the perspective of a continuum. On one end of the continuum, we have adultlike behavior. On the other end of the continuum, we have childlike behavior. Remember, one of the definitions of adultlike behavior is formal; and one of the definitions of childlike behavior is informal. Let's use those adjectives and build a continuum as shown in Figure 5–5.

When you first make a sales call, the environment is located on this continuum. You walk into a paneled office with lots of bookcases. The executive you are calling on is wearing a black suit, white shirt, and club tie. He sits behind a large desk. There is an oriental rug on the floor. Where would you place the sales situation? Would it be a 5? Is that an average sales environment for the community banker? What is an average environment? Is it adultlike and formal or childlike and informal?

Here's a bit of reality. Let's label each phase of this first encounter:

A. You walk into a retail store that is one block away from your branch. It is a pharmacy. The owner is behind the pharmacy counter. He is wearing a name tag on his white coat. He's balding and combs what's left over his bald spot. Half glasses.

B. He looks over his glasses and sees you approaching. He makes good eye contact with a warm smile.

C. "Mr. Savage?" you ask politely, at about 5 on the continuum.

D. "That's right," he responds in a pleasant outgoing way. "Can I help you?"

F I G U R E   5–5

Behavior Continuum

   E. "I'm Ted Willis from Willoweed National Bank. We talked on
   the phone this morning."
   F. "Sure Ted." He holds out his hand. "I'm pleased to meet you.
   Come on up. We can talk back here."

   Look at Figure 5–6 to see how that brief beginning moved along the
continuum. It started on the formal side of the continuum (A). The pharmacy, white and austere. Then (B) the personality of the pharmacist
showed through in his smile. The salesperson positioned himself right in
the middle (C). The pharmacist responded in a more informal way (D).
The salesperson maintained his position (E). The pharmacist moved the
momentum (F).

   Now, you as a salesperson must understand that you have the power
to control the movement on that continuum. Watch your customer and listen to her. You psychologically position yourself close to your customer.
If, for example, you were not aware of fluctuating personality styles and
you happened to be a very informal person meeting a very formal person,
you might start out wearing your Hawaiian shirt and sandals. Your customer is in a black suit. You say, "Hey there, How ya doin'?"

   He says, "I'm fine."

   The difference between those two personalities is called the degree
of discomfort in that encounter. (See Figure 5–7.) The customer does not
feel comfortable. Actually, I think it would be safe to say that the customer doesn't even like you very much. No trust. No comfort. People buy
products from people they feel comfortable with. Products do not sell
themselves. People sell products.

   So back to the original premise. Effective selling requires a high
degree of sensitivity to the concept of trust and comfort. You must build
it with your customer.

F I G U R E   5–6

Degree of Comfort

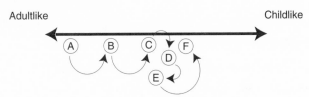

F I G U R E   5–7

Degree of Discomfort

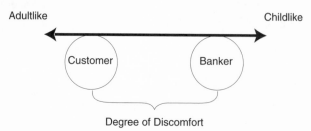

Degree of Discomfort

The question that must be in the forefront of your mind at this point is, Well this all fine. You want me to change my behavior and all; but what specifically do I change?

Let's go back to the beginning. We discovered that there are three parts to total communications: body language, tone, and voice. Following is a more dramatic way to look at it :

1. The choreography (the visual parts).

2. The music (the auditory parts).

3. The lyrics (the words).

The thrill of a musical is all encompassing when you sit in the audience because you are exposed to all the variables of communications. You are being bombarded by visual and auditory stimuli, and it takes you in completely.

Selling is communications, and it is like a stage production. A good salesperson must be as aware of his sales process, as a producer is aware of her musical. And like the original hypothesis, the first two parts, choreography and music, account for 87 percent of the total effect. Lyrics are 13 percent.

Why do so many people go to the opera when they can't even understand the language? Why do so many people go to High Masses in Latin when they don't speak the language? It's the choreography and the music. They get the point across.

In sales, it's the same. We can delve into those three areas and pinpoint certain characteristics:

Choreography: How you look and move throughout the communication processes. And how your customer looks and moves.

Music: At what rate and volume your message is delivered.

Lyrics: Exactly what you say.

As you can see from the Figure 5–8, 10 variables enable communications to be either adultlike or childlike. Looked at in another way, here are 10 variables you will have to regulate changing your behavior from adultlike to childlike behavior.

They are divided into three parts: choreography, music, and lyrics. Those characteristics that are more visual or physical we call choreography. Those characteristics that have to do with the auditory tone of your voice we call music. Those things that have to do with the actual words we call lyrics.

Let's examine the characteristics not so much to mimic the behavior of our customers and, therefore, look foolish, but rather to modify our own behavior ever so slightly and progressively, thus making our customers feel more comfortable around us.

Choreography Traits

Physical Contact We find that adultlike people shy away from physical contact—from affection. They are not huggers. The more adultlike a person is, the more uncomfortable he or she is with physical contact. From a business point of view, adultlike people prefer firm, quick handshakes. They don't like back patters and people who touch their elbows while they are talking. Women who keep touching an adultlike male will send the wrong signal, whereas a childlike male can react casually to a casual, harmless female touch.

I am fairly informal. My writing style is informal, I am sure you would agree. Yet I am not a hugger; even socially I am not comfortable with it. My wife is a hugger. She hugs the Lickfields, Tammy and Bill, when they visit us socially. I don't hug Bill; it doesn't feel right. I hug Tammy because I'm supposed to, but I don't like to hug for a long time. You know, just a polite hug and a pretend kiss. Even though I exhibit many informal characteristics, I still have formal characteristics. Few people are totally formal or totally informal.

If you are a salesperson and your customer is obviously formal, don't pat him on the back or participate in a lingering handshake.

Space Limitations Space limitations are closely related to physical contact, or how close you stand to someone. When you are too close,

F I G U R E   5–8

Musical Traits and Communication Styles

Choreography

Communication Style	Physical Contact	Space Limitations	Postures	Gestures	Clothes Styles
FORMAL (Adultlike)	Brief, firm handshakes. Avoids physical contact. Don't hug!	Needs large space. Keeps a distance from other people. Likes large rooms.	Closed, rigid, straight.	Few gestures. Deliberate and jabbing when used.	Neutral with high authority. Dark suits, and so on.
INFORMAL (Childlike)	Lingering, soft handshakes. Back patter. Hugger!	Needs very little space. Stands close when talking. Likes cozy little rooms.	Open, relaxed, "S" shaped.	Many gestures aimless in nature. Lots of head movements.	Loose unbuttoned. Leisure type. Loafers.

Music   ### Lyrics

Communication Style	Rate	Volume	Language Selection	Organization	Topics
FORMAL (Adultlike)	Deliberate.	Medium to loud.	Many multi- syllable words. Specific, technical terms. Frequent use of business buzz words.	Primacy.	Accomplishment. Performance
INFORMAL (Childlike)	Medium to slow.	Medium to soft.	Many one- syllable words. Many personal references. Sometimes vague or confusing. Lots of in dialogue. Slang.	Recency.	Belonging. Confiding. Sharing.

your customer gives you signals, such as backing away or losing eye contact. The customer looks away, glancing occasionally out of the corner of her eyes. Such behavior is very awkward and sends definite signals.

Adultlike people need space. They like large rooms, big offices, big desks. They are comfortable when you are on one side of the desk and they are on the other. If you are an adultlike salesperson, you are comfortable when your prospect asks you to sit in a large, straight-backed chair opposite her desk, with the formal customer sitting on the other side of the desk. A childlike person in that exact situation feels uncomfortable, stiff, and keeps glancing at the sofa and comfortable chair at the other end of the opulent office.

Childlike customers prefer sofas and conversation clusters in their offices. Professional decorators tell executives that they should have clusters of comfortable chairs in their offices to put other employees and guests at ease when they visit. So a formal executive will have half of the office dedicated to a large sofa, coffee table (with copies of *Fortune, Business Week, The Wall Street Journal, The New Yorker*), and two comfy chairs. Strangely enough, the executive would prefer to sit at his desk . . . and rarely reads *The New Yorker.*

Space Adultlike people demand it. When you violate that space, your customer is not comfortable.

Posture Adultlike people stand straight. They hold their shoulders back and tend to sit upright as if they would be just as comfortable without a back on their chairs. Childlike people relax physically. They are comfortable scooting down in their chairs, crossing their legs in what my kids call the figure-four configuration. Very informal people almost appear to be sitting on their backs in a chair, spreading their feet out in a relaxed manner.

With informal childlike customers, be careful not to be terribly rigid since informal people are very sensitive to formal postures. That doesn't mean you should totally mimic the customer. I don't believe in that because if you are very formal and you try to become very informal, it will appear insincere or faked. Your customer spots it in an instant and becomes turned off.

Gestures Adultlike people gesture from their hips. It's as if their elbows were glued to their hips. They make small, swift, chopping gestures. They frequently develop nervous gestures like straightening their ties or unbuttoning and buttoning their jackets. Informal people make large wide gestures. Speech coaches call it pin-wheeling, that flailing, extended arm movement we see from time to time.

Again, I caution you not to use this information to mimic but to realize there are gradations of these characteristics. If you are formal and making a sales call on an informal customer, it just means that you soften your physical signals. Don't feel so confined physically. Relax a bit more.

Dress   Dress is a very important characteristic, especially from a sales point of view. Rightly or wrongly, business etiquette is severely influenced by how you dress. We tend to think someone is more successful if they wear dark suits, white shirts, polished shoes. If your customer is dressed stylishly and you are dressed casually with camping boots, your customer will remember you as a bit unorganized, sloppily dressed, and so on. Even though we know that isn't true, the image that is left will manifest itself in a negative way with your customer.

Childlike people are not as influenced by how someone is dressed as adultlike people. If you are calling on a contractor and he is wearing jeans and boots and an open-neck shirt, you can wear a black suit. You should. If you are going to be a banker, you should be a banker. You can always take off your jacket as you tour the plant or farm, but your uniform is that of a banker. So that makes this one characteristic easy. Dress the way bankers are perceived to look . . . whether your customers are formal or informal.

Music Traits

Rate   Childlike people talk slowly. They let their words drag out. It's interesting how southerners are perceived by northerners and vice versa. Northerners perceive southerners as informal. Southerners perceive northerners as formal. A lot of that has to do with the rate of delivery. Nice, easy, slow, laid-back speech versus harsh, fast, intense speech—the difference between adultlike and childlike.

Volume   In general terms, adultlike people speak louder than childlike people. It is interesting to look at the great orators; they seemed to shout. The truth of the matter is that 50 years ago they had to shout because there was no amplification system. Consider Lenin, a truly great orator, speaking to 50,000 Soviets in 1922. He screamed! He had to! There was no PA system. But, culturally, that left us with the stereotype of the formal leader speaking loudly.

Today, we find many formal leaders who speak quietly, for example, President Ronald Reagan spoke quietly. Even though many think Reagan was adultlike, I believe he was a very informal president. His humor, his delivery while sitting at his desk chatting with the American people was informal, childlike. President Richard Nixon was informal. Prime Minister Margaret Thatcher was formal. Both used strong volume in their delivery. Jimmy Carter was informal; his volume was very quiet.

Lyrics Traits

Language Selection   While we are on the subject of Jimmy Carter. Consider his name: Jimmy. Not James, Jimmy. From the beginning, he positioned himself as informal. He wanted to differentiate himself from Nixon. His name was informal from the outset. In one of his earlier campaign commercials, he stated, "I'll never lie to ya." His language was informal; lots of slang, personal references, and so forth.

Organization   An interesting concept, organization has to do with how people prioritize information within the context of a thought. Some people, when they deliver a message, structure the content of that message in a passive, painless (sometimes evasive) way. Others deliver that same message in a direct (sometimes painful) way. These two styles of delivery are referred to as primacy and recency.

If I am asked a question and answer it in a straightforward, direct fashion, I am said to deliver information in primacy. In Figure 5–9, we show the primacy delivery. The answer (or singleness of purpose of the dialogue) is stated at the beginning. We have a tendency to use primacy when we deliver good news. It is much easier to do that.

"Did we get the account?"

"Yes. Thanks to your hard work, the extra effort from computer resources, and the support of the marketing department."

From a management point of view, primacy is extremely important. If managers are supposed to manage, then they must deliver information in a totally clear, direct fashion; no beating around the bush.

FIGURE 5—9

Primacy Delivery

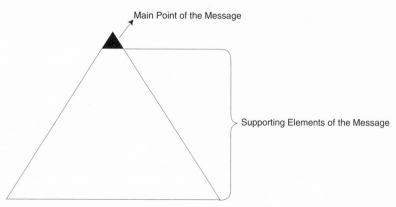

In Figure 5–10, we show recency.

This is the way we traditionally deliver bad information. We hem and haw and beat around the bush to the point that sometimes we never deliver the information at all. Psychologically, we hope the person knows what we mean. It might go something like this:

"Did we get the account?"

"It's not absolutely final, at this point. I mean, you know how companies are; they make a decision one way one time and another way 10 minutes later. I mean, really, when you think about what we are offering versus our competition, we're head and shoulders above the rest. The staff really did a great job on the presentation especially the computer and marketing folks. Fantastic job!"

The real relevancy of this occurs in a sales situation when it becomes obvious that you need to know where you are. "How am I doing?" you want to ask. "Can we do business? Yes or No?" But we don't ask. We beat around the bush. If you are with a formal adultlike client, you can ask. Formal people prefer to deal in primacy. They get confused with recency. You send the wrong message to a formal person if you are not direct.

In Figure 5–11 you can see both primacy and recency in the context of a direct question, "Do you like my new car?"

How you answer questions and how you deliver information is critical to the sales process. If you are an informal person, you will find primacy a difficult (even awkward) style to adapt. If you want to be a good manager,

F I G U R E   5–10

Recency Delivery

however, you absolutely need to perfect primacy management techniques. As a branch manager, your staff depends on you to tell them exactly what is going on. You need to decide what that information is and how to deliver it.

Topics What do adultlike and childlike people like to talk about? Adultlike people tend toward accomplishments. They like to talk about the end result, the bottom line. Did they get it or not? Childlike people like to talk about the process. How did they get to the end result? What did it feel like? Who was involved?

Now go back to page 68 and look at Figure 5–8 again. From a sales point of view, you will find yourself able to make slight changes in 4 to 6 of the 10 characteristics. That is all that is expected, since your adjustment to your customer's style must be gradual and smooth. There is a transition time when you realize that your existing style would not be totally comfortable for your customer, so you make certain, specific changes.

Physical contact is an easy one to change. So are space and dress. Rate and volume are difficult to adjust in a sales encounter. Failure to do them right comes off as affected. You can work on those two during a sales presentation versus a sales call.

Language selection, organization, and topics are all characteristics you can change during a sales call and during a sales presentation. As you can tell, these characteristics are also very important parts of your management style and ability to react effectively to your staff.

F I G U R E   5–11

Primacy and Recency Deliveries

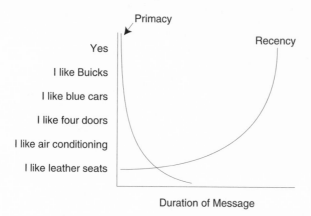

Duration of Message

Many communication techniques used in the sales process are applicable in the management process. One area we have not spent a great deal of time on is the angry customer or the angry employee; in other words, dealing with conflict. Conflict is created in a parentlike state. Customers who are unhappy want to talk at you. They expect you to listen and not talk. Emotion is obvious. All of this applies also to your staff. From time to time, you end up with an angry staff member in your office complaining about something that is going wrong in the branch. The way you handle employee conflict and customer conflict is very similar because it manifests itself as parentlike behavior, sometimes verging on childlike behavior.

The more you study transactional analysis, the closer parentlike and childlike behaviors appear to be. Both are emotional behaviors. Adultlike is the only behavior that is not emotional. Parentlike and childlike are both swing behaviors, meaning that the mood of the behavior can be changed quickly. Volatility is apparent in both behaviors. The major difference is that childlike is two-way communication and parentlike is one-way communication. Don't deal with parentlike behavior in a parentlike way because it is considered to be a two-way communication style.

Parentlike behavior is exhibited by the angry customer or the angry employee who storms into your office. It is exhibited even by the belligerent, rude customer you meet during an external sales call. They are all exhibiting parentlike behavior verging toward childlike behavior.

Sometimes the behavior is not quite as obvious and it builds. These traits characterize impending conflict:

Folded arms

Lowered head

Clenched teeth

Abrupt head movements

Fast, deliberate walk

Noticeable fidgeting

Sighs

Resting on one foot, then the other

Crossing and uncrossing of legs

Hands on hips

Constantly seeking eye contact

Narrowing of eyes

Looks of exasperation

If you watch the person with whom you are communicating, the signals are very clear. The one central behavioral tool to use, as soon as possible, is diffusion of the emotion. Get rid of the anger or get it into perspective so you can deal with it.

The way out of parentlike behavior is through adultlike behavior, but only after dealing with the emotion first. Then the classic adultlike traits can be applied, for example, order, logic, and so on.

Getting rid of emotion requires concentration. You have to make a mental pause and, for an instant, step back and refocus on the person. The process of conflict resolution is

Focus ⟶ Apologize ⟶ Investigate ⟶ Satisfy

The first thing to do when you find yourself entering into a conflict is *focus* on the person implementing the conflict. That means concentrate and visually establish firm eye contact in a nonthreatening, nonchallenging way.

Have you ever watched the teller line when an irate customer walks up to a teller and starts chewing her out? The teller will lower her eyes and purposely lose eye contact. Psychologically, we do the old ostrich trick. If we can't see the danger, then the danger can't see us; therefore, it doesn't exist. Losing eye contact gives the angered customer more courage and he begins to believe that he can get away with this absurd behavior. So he gets more belligerent. Focusing on the person under conflict requires concentration and steadiness. You should look concerned, not bored, not angry—concerned.

Now it is time to defuse the emotion. *Apologize.* Not in the middle of the tirade. Let the customer run with his anger while you focus. At the first opportunity to respond, use the word, *Sorry.*

"Mr. Johnson, I'm very sorry."

"Mrs. Winslow, on behalf of the bank I am sorry."

"On behalf of my staff, I would like to apologize and assure you that we can get this straightened out."

"I am sorry."

The English language somehow connotes wrongful doing with *sorry.* Also we believe sorry implies that we won't do it again.

According to the dictionary, sorry means "regret for loss, mournful disappointment." It doesn't say anything about being to blame or wrong. Often we don't want to apologize because we didn't do anything wrong! How many times have we heard that? Sorry does not mean that you did anything wrong. For that matter, it does not mean that you won't do it again. During the 28 years I've been married, I have really learned how to apologize!

There is a cycle of anger in which the diffusing element of anger is the psychological reward. That reward can be "I'm sorry." In Figure 5–12, anger is looking for someone to blame (that's you!). The customer needs justice and that justice is the reward you will be giving by saying, "I'm sorry."

Too often, we counter the customer's anger with anger of our own. Or we disavow anything to do with the problem. "That's not my responsibility," we naively state, hoping that the customer will say, "Oh gosh, I'm sorry. Who should I see?" Let's be practical, here!

Telling a customer that it isn't your responsibility will only add to his anger and eventually you will become angry at the customer because of the verbal abuse you will be receiving. "Hey, buster. Don't talk to me that way!" you say.

Once you have dissipated the anger, you can then figure out just what made the person so angry in the first place. You do that through *investigation.* You will notice your customer's anger subsiding slightly. At that point, you offer your help.

FIGURE 5-12

The Cycle of Anger

"Mr. Johnson, let me see your April statement and see if there is anything I can do to solve this immediately."

Another approach might be, "Now, Mr. Arnold tell me how this happened so I can make sure it won't happen again."

You need to force your customer to think in an orderly, organized way, because by doing that you are forcing him into adultlike behavior.

Finally, when you have determined what the problem really is, you *satisfy* your customer by resolving the conflict in a way that your customer can clearly understand.

SUMMARY

1. A good salesperson listens 100 percent of the time and talks 10 percent.

2. There are three elements to communicating: body language, tone, and words. All three total 100 percent of the communication process. Research has shown that the most important part of communication is body language, which accounts for 55 percent of the total. Tone accounts for 23 percent and words, 22 percent.

3. The three kinds of sales situations are win-win, lose-win, and lose-lose.

4. Your job, as a salesperson, is to create trust and comfort. It results in win-win sales. Repeat business, respect, and enjoyment of your job are the by-products of this kind of selling.

5. Transactional analysis defines three styles of communication: adultlike, parentlike, and childlike.

6. People buy products from people with whom they feel comfortable. Products do not sell themselves; people sell products.

7. Ten characteristics enable communications to be either formal or informal:

Physical contact	Rate
Space limitation	Volume
Posture	Language selection
Gestures	Organization
Dress	Topics

8. The two styles of delivery are primacy (straightforward and direct) and recency (beating around the bush.)

9. The process of conflict resolution is FOCUS, APOLOGIZE, INVESTIGATE, and SATISFY

CHAPTER 6

How to Ask Questions That Your Customer Wants to Answer

I've been in the communications business for almost 30 years professionally. Before that I was in it personally: verbally convincing my mother to change my diapers, picking on my brothers, falling in love, and so on. In 1961, I decided to really study this idea of writing and talking. . . and stuff.

When I graduated from college, I got a job writing advertising and "sales promotional" material. I had no idea what sales promotional material was. I couldn't have cared less. I wanted to write television commercials. But I had to do my apprenticeship and struggle through that kind of material.

That was when I began to learn about "the customer," that elusive thing salespeople called on. It was as if the customer were inanimate, something we were never allowed to see or meet for fear of being eaten alive!

I envisioned this customer as a male in his mid-50s. He was overweight. He had graying hair, balding on the top. Combed over the bald spot. Gray, three-piece suit. He never wore a coat. He had a bow tie. There were underarm stains on his white, poorly ironed shirt. In other words, the customer had a really rotten disposition. That was who I was writing for.

The sales force, back then, told me about customers. I heard all the war stories. It was as if they were the enemy.

Then someone in the sales department suggested that the kid who's writing the promotional stuff has to go to a sales training class. "He doesn't know what he's talking about," the guy said.

From that point, the veil of anonymity had been lifted from the customer. The customer was me as it turns out. In this chapter, you will learn to establish levels of comfort with yourself and others. You will learn how to ask questions people want to answer. Once you learn how to ask the right kinds of questions, then the people with whom you are talking will feel at ease with whom they are talking. When people feel comfortable they talk. So a good communicator's job is to get the other person to talk; get that person to talk about what he or she wants to talk about—not necessarily the product. It isn't the product that is important. Especially in sales.

NEEDS-BASED SELLING

The need is important in sales communication. The product or service can satisfy the need. So we must uncover the need. That means you must learn how to ask those kinds of questions that will eventually lead to statements regarding needs. Personal financial needs. Business financial needs. Those are the needs we will focus on.

If you are calling on a business prospect as a branch manager, you must aim the direction of the conversation toward the customer's needs. First, the personal needs (if he or she is informal), then the business financial needs.

What makes this idea of uncovering the need so difficult is that customers, in many cases, don't know exactly what their financial needs are.

What would happen if you were to start out a sales call by asking, "Tell me, Mrs. Blackstone, what are your financial needs?"

You might get a blank stare or a comment like, "Money."

Many corporations have carefully analyzed their business and through a business plan or series of planning meetings have uncovered specific areas of financial needs. But they don't know the bank's products like you do. Also, from a business point of view, you are sensitive to the issue of "protection," that is, protecting your bank from their inability to repay. Customers are aware of protection, but it is not as high on their priority list as it is on yours.

Being a business person, banking customer, and borrower, I tend to look at the growth of my company differently than my banker. Because it is my business, I am also more committed than my banker. I will work harder and sacrifice more than my banker. . . who is on a salary and refuses to meet me in my office at 6:00 AM! This is not to denigrate my banker. People who run businesses or own them are a different breed from those who work for a business. In most cases, our vision is clouded by a false sense of reality. If we were right, we make a lot of money. If we are wrong, we lose our house!

So this entire issue of needs becomes an overriding issue in learning how your customer thinks.

Your customer's needs are not the bank's products.

Your customer's needs are things like the following:

1. Short-term money based on receivables.
2. A method of earning money on money while it is not being used.
3. Assistance with payroll.
4. Funding a new venture at least financial risk.
5. Fitting employees into a retirement program.
6. How much is (symbol)23,000 today?
7. Saving money to make the bottom line look better.
8. Financial alternatives.
9. Courage to expand.
10. Spending more time with the family.

Your business customer does not "need" a business checking account.

Your business customer needs the most cost-efficient place to put money so as to carry on day-to-day business.

What your business customer really needs is an intuitive ear that can respond with some sound financial advice based on the overall picture. That is why I included numbers 9 and 10. They are very much needs. Especially number 10; a sensitivity to personal issues makes you more valuable to your client.

Business is made and driven by human beings. They all have personalities that affect their ability to do the job correctly. Understanding the personal factors that affect your client helps you become a better financial advisor. While companies change banks all the time; they don't change good financial advisors.

So you must learn to become more than an order taker. You must learn to become a financial advisor. You must become part of the infrastructure of your business clients. That means building trust and comfort.

You must learn how to get your business customer to open up and talk; talk about his business life and the factors that affect its growth and decline.

THE QUESTIONING OVERVIEW

Making a conversation happen is much like driving a car in January in Minnesota. You get yourself ready to start your car. Then you go out through the snow and get into the car. Next you start it. It runs a bit awkward, at first. So you let it idle briefly. Then you put it in gear and start driving. If you warmed it up properly, the car runs smoothly. You get to your destination. Then you turn off the ignition.

One can divide that process into separate parts. Similarly, one can divide a conversation into parts, as follows:

1. Preparation
2. Physical encounter
3. Introductory probe
4. Content momentum
5. Ending

These five parts to creating a conversation equate well to a sales communication process. We are talking about a smooth, comfortable conversation where the direction and momentum of the conversation are totally controlled by you. It's a conversation that happens to be business-related from a longer-term perspective.

Americans are short-term. That's why we have developed such an awkward sales position. We don't take our time. The Germans like to familiarize first. It's a custom. It's polite. The French get right to business. The Japanese take inordinate time in what they refer to as the developmental process of an encounter. The Irish are polite but they do like to get to business with few niceties.

The American culture has become short-term. It hasn't always been that way. Of late, we have become ensconced with a sense of urgency and our reaction has been to view business as business and personal as personal. When we decided to do that, we took the heart out of the sales process. Now it is get in there and get that order. Then get out!

Slow down!

The Process of Questioning

The concept that creates a conversation consists of one person who is truly interested in what he or she is talking about and another person who is also interested in what that person is talking about. That might be a real mental adjustment for you to make. You have to be the person who is also interested in what that person is talking about. That means you keep the conversation going. You must concentrate and control the pulse of the conversation. You can carry the conversation in and out of one topic at will.

Direct Questions and Open-Ended Questions

There are basically two kinds of questions. One type gets the conversation going. These questions are generally short and are part of a series of short questions that build as the content becomes focused.

These questions are direct questions because they require short answers, maybe one or two words.

QUESTION: "How ya doin'?"

ANSWER: "Fine, thanks."

QUESTION: "You from around here?"

ANSWER: "No. Pennsylvania."

QUESTION: "Just visiting?"

ANSWER: "Sort of. We will be moving here."

QUESTION: "No kidding. Soon?"

ANSWER: "We hope so. My company is moving me."

QUESTION: "Who do you work for?"

These questions are called direct questions. Short, concise, and progressive; one question leads to another. It can go too far.

1. "How ya doin'?"
   "Fine, thanks."
2. "You from around here?"
   "No. Pennsylvania."
3. "Just visiting?"
   "Sort of. We will be moving here."
4. "No kidding. Soon?"
   "We hope so. My company is moving me."

5. "Who do you work for?"
   "Johnson Electric."
6. "Oh, I know them. Up on Elm Street."
   "Yes. That's them."
7. "That's quite some company. They've got a fine reputation."
   "We have been pretty profitable."
8. "What do you do for them?"
   "Marketing."
9. "You mean advertising?"
   "Well, advertising is part of it."
10. "So you're going to be moving your family up here."
    "Yes."
11. "You have children?"
    "Three. Two boys and a girl."
12. "Will any of them go to our local high school?"
    "My oldest son."

Too many direct questions make the persons you are talking to uncomfortable.

Once again, read the conversation with the numbered questions. This time, circle the number where the conversation begins to be uncomfortable.

Where did the conversation become awkward? Some people have circled as early as number 5. Other people believe that conversation is still going smoothly at 12.

My feeling is number 7. That was the point at which something else needed to happen. The conversation became too one-sided and an element of awkwardness set in.

The opposite of direct questions is open-ended questions. Open-ended questions are questions that cannot be answered with one word. Open-ended questions are thought-provoking questions. They force the mind to process and compare data and then respond verbally.

Opening phrases such as "Tell me" or "Could you explain the difference between" or "How do you feel about" are all open-ended questions. Continuing statements or words such as "Why?" or "Go ahead" or "What do you mean by?" are all forcing an open-ended conversation to continue.

Those are the two kinds of questions: direct and open-ended. Those kinds of questions exist within a context that allows for trust and comfort.

That context has three distinct phases: (1) chatter, (2) intellect, and (3) emotion. Those phases represent the three stages you as a questionee will go through. Here is an example:

1. I ask you, "What do you like most about your job?"
   You answer quickly, "The people."
2. I continue the questioning process. "What else?"
   You think a little longer this time. "The, uh, challenge."
3. I continue the direction, "Go ahead. What else?"
   You frown slightly. Then chuckle, "Whadaya mean?"

The first question was easy to answer. You don't really have to think. That's like someone asking, "How ya doin'?" That's easy. We call questions like that chatter. They do not require a real mental process. Chatter is direct questions.

The second question was a little more difficult. It forced you to think, to use your mental processes. Actually, your mind began using another dimension of itself; it canned available information. It processed and compared. (Honestly, that's what your mind does when it starts working.) That mental process of questioning is called intellect, or open-ended questions.

When the mind begins to work, it is forced to do so by questions that require some thinking. Those kind of questions are open-ended questions. The questioning process involved in open-ended questions is intellect. Here is how an open-ended question would have made the dialogue on page 83 more comfortable. I will insert an open-ended question after direct question 6 and force intellect as follows:

1. "How ya doin'?"
   "Fine, thanks."
2. "You from around here?"
   "No. Pennsylvania."
3. "Just visiting?"
   "Sort of. We will be moving here."
4. "No kidding. Soon?"
   "We hope so. My company is moving me."
5. "Who do you work for?"
   "Johnson Electric."
6. "Oh, I know them. Up on Elm Street. Tell me what, exactly, do you make?"

"We make electrical relays and customized electrical compo-
nents."

7. "You lost me, there. As a consumer, where would I see something Johnson makes?"
"In a lot of places. For example, almost every electrical tool
you have has some kind of relay or component that we make.
Your electric fans, kitchen appliances, everything."

8. "How'd ya ever get into that kind of business?"

Can you see how the conversation began to rely more on the questionee versus the questionor? From a sales point of view, the questionee
would be the salesperson. The questionor would be the customer.

Good salespeople listen. Good customers talk. Really good salespeople make good customers talk. Returning to chatter, intellect, and
emotion, now you have seen chatter. You understand that it is direct questions. You also understand its limitations, that is, too many direct questions make the questionee uncomfortable.

You have also learned about intellect. It is forced or allowed to happen through open-ended questions. Good conversations rely on the interplay of direct and open-ended questions because those two force the mental process of intellect.

What about emotion? Emotion is what happens when you do too
much chatter, too many direct questions. Also, emotion comes about for
salespeople when their questions are not customer-sensitive. Here's a
good example:

BANKER: "Hi, Tom. How are you?"

CUSTOMER: "Just fine, Mary."

BANKER: "I really appreciate your giving me a few minutes."

CUSTOMER: "No problem. Always willing to talk to bankers."

BANKER: "So how is your business doing, Tom?"

CUSTOMER: "Not bad considering the economy."

BANKER: "I know. This economy can get to just about every
industry if you're not careful. Are your sales down?"

CUSTOMER: "Not below what we forecasted."

BANKER: "What were they last month?"

CUSTOMER: "Oh, I dunno. Probably around a $185 K."

BANKER: "How much of that can you put in your own pocket?"

CUSTOMER: "Gee, Mary. I'm not sure that's any of your business."

Emotion is not only the number of direct questions you ask, but the kind of questions you ask. If you are aware of business and the kinds of things that are acceptable business dialogue, you won't step over your bounds.

Sometimes you can turn off clients and you are not really aware of it. If you watch your clients, however, they will give you signals. They suddenly decide they are running out of time. Or they begin arguing with you. They look at their watches or lose eye contact with you. Customer sensitivity is an art. If you concentrate on the customer, you will become better at it. Emotion is where a conversation should not go. If, in fact, people buy products from people they feel comfortable with, emotion clogs the comfort zone and a sale cannot happen.

In Figure 6–1 you can see the three kinds of selling looked at from the perspective of chatter, intellect, and emotion.

A truly effective sales encounter never gets into emotion. It also does not stay in chatter very long. The secret to an effective conversation is one that resides in intellect for the major part of the time.

What are the three types of sales encounters represented by the three different curves (in Figure 6–1)? In sales encounter number 1, there was

F I G U R E   6–1

Effects of These Types of Sales Questions During
Three Sales Encounters

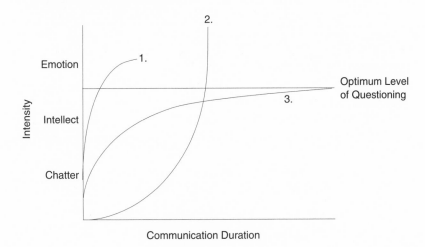

very little chatter and practically no intellect. That encounter might have been one opening statement by the salesperson such as "Are you here to buy or just to look around?"

In sales encounter number 2, it got into emotion because there was too much chatter. The conversation never got around to where it was supposed to be. It was one of those conversations where the salesperson just kept asking questions that obviously were going nowhere.

Sales encounter number 3 works well. A brief period of chatter followed by a long period of intellect without ever going into emotion. Bravo!

Structured Questions

Now that we know how to ask questions in general, we should learn how to ask questions that are specifically related to banking products and services. We call those structured questions. You will learn in the following chapter how those questions fit into the overall sales process. For now, let's trace some questions in a sales process to determine how structured business questions allow the good salesperson to determine the customer's financial needs.

Let's use specific situations to describe this questioning. For example, you are going to make a first call on the local pharmacist. After you go through the personal probing, you will want to find out about the pharmacy business. You do so by setting up some qualifying questions. We call these questions closed probes. Because closed probes ask for specifics, they are similar to direct questions. These probes are carefully planned and lead to conclusions. They also are used to verify information.

In the local pharmacy, after I had spend some time learning about the owner and his family, I might say, "Mr. Smith, I would imagine that you would feel more comfortable dealing with a bank that had a basic understanding of your business, wouldn't you?"

"Well, yes. That would be helpful. But I couldn't expect my banker to become an authority on the retail druggist business."

"It certainly would make it easier on us, as your banker, to loan you money if we understood some basics of your business. Wouldn't you agree?"

"Well, yes. I would agree with that."

"Is there, for example, an industry average margin that you are familiar with?"

"Well, I am a member of the National Association of Retail Druggists. They do have those kinds of figures."

"I certainly would like to become more familiar with your industry. Does this association have a book or pamphlet that I might read?"

"As a matter of fact, they do. I've got one over here. I happened to be going through it the other day. Let's see." He browses through a stack of magazines and papers. "Ah, here it is. This might be helpful."

"Would you mind if I borrowed that? I will get it back to you as soon as I finish."

"Sure. I don't see why not. You know this business doesn't make a big margin."

"Few retailers are making big margins these days. I guess it's the ongoing struggle to increase sales and decrease expenses."

"Easy to say."

Now the pharmacist is ready to talk if I ask the right questions. The questions that ask for more information or expansion are called open probes. Open probes are similar to open-ended questions. They literally force the customer to elaborate on an issue. Like open-ended questions, they sometimes start with "Tell me." Let's get back to the conversation with the pharmacist and see how they work.

"I'm sure you're right. I sit there in my comfortable little branch with a salary; it is difficult for me to understand what real accountability is."

"Well, if I had to do it over again, I'd probably do the same thing."

"Tell me, Mr. Smith, what are the variables in your business that impact your bottom line . . . like payroll or rent?"

"Well, first of all, the druggist industry is choked with an average margin of somewhere in the 21 to 23 percent area and. . ."

Now the pharmacist is talking; he feels like an authority. You know the direction that you will be steering the conversation. You could even be taking notes. He's be flattered.

Using a combination of informal questioning and structured questioning, makes the prospect feel comfortable enough to talk about finances. The sales model discussed in the next chapter graphically illustrates how these two parts of business questioning enable the salesperson to assess a prospect's true financial needs.

The following expanded sales example shows how a banker finds the kind of information needed and uses it to make the customer feel at ease: Allison D'Arrigo is a branch manager for a $900 million bank in the northeast. She has been developing a relationship with a prospective client for the past several months. She sent a letter. Followed up with a phone call. Now she has had two meetings. Allison has learned a lot about her potential customer. His name is Isaac Adamson. He owns a company that provides homes and services for individuals with traumatic brain injuries. When she first met him, she didn't really want to talk about his business because it seemed like such a sensitive thing. But as time passed, she learned a little about it. She learned a lot about Adamson.

He's married and has two children; Mary Alice is 12 and Jonathon, 9. Adamson plays a lot of tennis and is a fitness fanatic. Gets up early every morning and runs three miles. He usually works out at a Nautilus center three times a week. A local person, he attended the local high school and went to the state university.

Adamson got into the business because his brother Peter was seriously injured in an automobile accident 20 years ago. His family had cared for him until he became a serious burden; they were ill-equipped to handle Peter's handicap.

Peter's injury was covered by an insurance settlement that Adamson put into a family trust fund. The money from the family trust would provide the kind of assistance and lodging Peter would need.

Adamson began getting extremely involved in just exactly what adequate supervision meant for traumatic brain injury patients. Who provided it? How much did it cost? How good was it supposed to be? As he got more and more knowledgeable, other families or friends of people with traumatic brain injury contacted him. Adamson stayed very involved in the National Head Injury Foundation and participated in local support groups.

In 1975, Adamson purchased a home for Peter. He used some of Peter's funds as the down payment. When he bought the home, another family had asked if their son could live at that home with Peter. Both had a similar level of head injury and did not need 24-hour live-in supervision. The trust fund monies from Peter and the other individual adequately covered the mortgage and the periodic help needed to satisfactorily care for the two handicapped men.

At present, Adamson rents three homes to individuals who have varying degrees of head injuries. Adamson runs a very profitable, reputable business. He wants to expand greatly at this point. His next logical step would be to buy two homes at once and refurbish them for three patients.

His first three mortgages are with a local savings bank. He's happy with them. D'Arrigo and Adamson had the following structured conversation:

"Isaac, your three properties are with Blancharstown Savings?"

"That's right."

"Who has your home?"

"First Union."

"Is that an old mortgage?"

"Not really. I remortgaged to get the downpayment on property number three."

"Tell me your plans for financing the new properties."

"Well, I think I'm just going to follow traditional mortgage policies. I've got the 20 percent to put down. The monthly income from my patients should cover my total expenses."

"How much are the two new properties?" she asked.

"Front Street I can get for $175,000. Elm Street will probably run me $120,000, but it will need more work."

"Let's see. You are looking for around $300,000 plus refurbishing."

"That will cost another hundred grand."

"And you do have the $60,000 to put down."

"Oh, easily. If I have to."

"Do you have patients for the homes?"

"Allison, let me show you something. Here is a file of prospective patients, individuals waiting to be placed in excellent residential facilities like I offer. I've got more than 10 names. The projected income from just four individuals will pay a 25-year mortgage comfortably."

"Isaac, would you show me exactly how cash flow works in your business. I'd like to put together a package for the bank, but I will need a brief lesson."

"Sure. As a matter of fact, I've been pulling together some numbers to talk with my accountant."

What happened in that sales encounter was a deep awareness of Adamson's pride in his business combined with self-confidence on D'Arrigo's part to know that he would spend some time with her to explain his business. You see, once a prospective customer is willing to sit down and work on paper with you, you have broken through the comfort and trust levels. You develop solid relationships through questions not through sales pitches.

S U M M A R Y

1. A good communicator's job is to get the other person to talk about what that person wants to talk about, not the product. It isn't the product that is important. Especially in sales, it is the other person's needs.

2. Needs-based selling concentrates on the customer's needs rather than on the salesperson's product.

3. The five parts to a conversation are preparation, physical encounter, introductory probe, content momentum, and ending.

4. Direct questions require short answers of maybe one or two words.

5. Open-ended questions are thought-provoking questions. They force the mind to process and compare data and then respond verbally.

6. The three distinct phases of questioning are chatter, intellect, and emotion.

7. Good salespeople listen. Good customers talk. Really good salespeople make good customers talk.

8. Structured questions are questions that are specifically related to the business at hand.

9. Closed probes ask for specifics. They are similar to direct questions. These probes are carefully planned and lead to conclusions. They also are used to verify information.

10. Open probes are similar to open-ended questions. They literally force the customer to elaborate on an issue.

CHAPTER 7

Building a Sales Model

Performance-based behavior generally requires two people: One working toward a clear-cut goal and the other assisting in the goal or competing.

The baseball player works toward the goal of winning the game. He relies on his ability to understand and participate in a team effort. The concept of team surrounds his individual goals, for example, hitting the ball or catching the ball. The opponent has the same goals.

The track star works toward the goal of winning the race. She relies on her individual efforts to accomplish that goal, for example, starting the race, running the race and finishing the race. She does not rely on team effort per se, because she is the individual doing the running. Her opponents have the same goals.

Success at performance requires a team effort. The boxer relies on his trainer, his manager, his physician, his PR people. The basketball player relies on his or her teammates, as well as managers, trainers, and so on. The day of the lone individual solely pursuing a goal is gone.

These individuals or teams realize they must constantly improve. The tennis player who wins Wimbledon sets new standards of excellence against which all other tennis players are measured. The other tennis players analyze the winner's game in an attempt to win the next time.

Winning or losing becomes the end result. It is the means to that end result that allows the winners to win. So humans began analyzing the means to the end. Performance functions can be diagrammed so we can view the entire process we are analyzing; for example, the tennis player and the salesperson. From a broad, nonspecific point of view, Figure 7–1 shows a schematic model for a professional tennis player. First is the pre-match preparation. That means the conditioning, analyzing the opponents via video or in-person, endless practice sessions, and meetings with supporters, coaches, and trainers.

Second is the warm-up period with the person on the other side of the net. The tennis player has the opportunity to watch that person within the context of her own style. The tennis player looks for certain traits at this point. How does the person on the other side of the net handle harder strokes versus easy strokes? Side to side? How is the person on the other side of the net moving? Do I see anything I haven't seen before such as a new stroke? Is the person on the other side of the net fresh? Psyched? The warm-up is really to observe the person on the other side of the net.

Notice that I have refused to call the person on the other side of the net the opponent. I do that so we don't lose perspective of the upcoming analogy to the sales prospect. The prospect is not the opponent in a win-win situation.

Third, after the warm-up is the actual match. At this point, the tennis player should not be thinking about every detail of the stroke or sulking over missed shots. The successful player plays the match as best he can. Psychologically, the player keeps saying, "Just play your game. Have fun. Enjoy yourself. Look forward to hitting the ball. Don't think of the point. Think of the ball."

Fourth, after the match is over, the tennis player goes through a postmatch analysis to analyze the game with supporters.

Within the context of that match itself is the natural flow of the carefully rehearsed movements. Looking at Figure 7–2, note how the details of the process fit into the model. What I have done is to take the match and, within the actual match, break down the total stroke into its elements. That is what one does in the pursuit of continuous performance improvement; you break down the process into increments for analysis.

F I G U R E   7–1

Tennis Player's Performance

F I G U R E   7–2

Elements of the Total Stroke

Prematch Preparation	The Match Warm-up	The Match	Postmatch Analysis
Racquet Back	Position	Step into Ball	Stroke	The Follow-Through

THE SALES PROCESS

Now let's do the same thing for the sales process in Figure 7–3. The preapproach function is the time spent getting prepared. You analyze your market, network, and develop a list. You probably start some preapproach letters, so you can do phone calls soliciting an appointment. The introduction is like the warm-up in tennis. You meet the customer and chat, getting to know her style, what kind of a person she is, how the business is managed, family structure, and so on.

F I G U R E   7–3

Salesperson's Performance

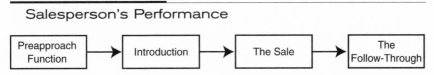

Then there is the sale. That is when you have determined it is time to get the customer thinking about solving some specific financial needs with the products or services that your bank has to offer.

The follow-through is sending out a thank you letter. If you made the sales call with an associate, you need to instantly debrief and reflect on what happened during the call. What were the strong parts? What were the weak parts? What will you need to do to keep the prospect alive?

Now let's consider an expanded sales model similar in design to the tennis model. Figure 7–4 has the same four main heads: preapproach function, introduction, the sale, and the follow-through. Now you can view everything that falls under those four basic headings. You can see the individual parts of a sales process, the means to the end.

FIGURE   7–4

Expanded Sales Model

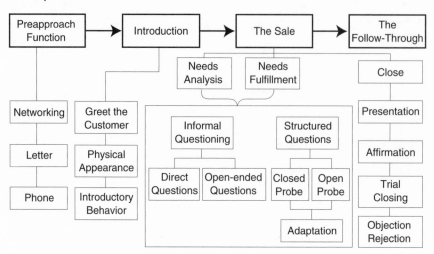

We will refer to the last diagram as our sales model. You read it from left to right, going vertically where indicated.

Although it appears quite complex, this model is very simple because it allows the viewer to internalize its elements at any desired level of complexity. The top boxes are the most general; the vertical boxes become more and more specific. We study this model by beginning at the left section of the diagram. (See Figure 7–5.)

FIGURE   7–5

Preapproach Function

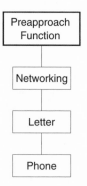

The Preapproach Function

The preapproach function is one part of this sales model that frequently does not appear in other sales models. If you remember our diagram from Chapter 3, page 42, the preapproach function is used very little in the hard-sales process. So any aggressive, hard selling does not rely, to any sizable degree, on the elements of this function.

The preapproach function entails knowing your market and doing a complete sales analysis of it. Networking, prospecting, customer information files, notes, and letters all are part of the preapproach function. We covered a lot of that in Chapter 4.

The Preapproach Letter

One particular part of the preapproach function is the preapproach letter. Many larger banks have these kinds of letters in a database, accessible through a word processing program. If you don't have preapproach letters in your computer files, then develop some rules for preapproach letters as well as some letters that are general enough that you can type in names and companies with maybe a sentence or two of customization. (See Figure 7–6.)

As a rule, the letter should never be more than one page. Never! If you are new to a community, the objective would be to introduce yourself by way of the bank. Indicate that you would like to call the person and perhaps stop by. If you received the name from another person, you should indicate who recommended that you call. If the name came from an association, you should indicate the name of the association. The letter should be short and to the point. For example:

January 3, 1995

Ms. Alice F. Marble
Pre-Cash Specialties, Inc.
145 Salem Street
Foxcroft, AR 20987

Dear Ms. Marble,

Recently, I joined the Willoweed Bank in Foxcroft as the branch manager. Naturally, the bank's commitment to community growth and progress includes

(continued)

---

an active interest in the Foxcroft Chamber. As an active member of the Chamber, you can appreciate the role of community banking in your business.

Over the next few weeks, as I become more familiar with the business community, I would appreciate the opportunity to stop by and visit with you briefly, just to introduce myself and the bank.

In the meantime, I have enclosed our most recent annual report for your perusal.

Sincerely,

John Williams
Branch Manager

Here is another approach, assuming you have received the name from another person.

January 1, 1995

Ms. Alice F. Marble
Pre-Cash Specialties, Inc.
145 Salem Street
Foxcroft, AR 20987

Dear Ms. Marble,

Last week I spoke with Dan Jordan at Riverside Products. He suggested that I get in touch with you since you were considering a warehouse expansion.

Recently, I joined the Willoweed Bank in Foxcroft as the business development officer. I am familiar with the success your company has enjoyed and would like to learn more about Pre-Cash Specialties in the event you might need some financial assistance or advice.

I am enclosing our most recent annual report for your perusal and will call you for an appointment within the next two weeks. Thank you for your consideration.

Sincerely,

John Williams
Business Development Officer

F I G U R E   7-6

Preapproach Letter

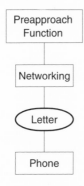

Short and to the point. A preapproach letter is not designed to sell any product or service. You only need to implant your name and associate that name with someone or some organization that the person knows.

You should either send an annual report or recent press clipping with the preapproach letter. In that way, the mailing has a little bit more substance so it will get past the secretary.

Totally unsolicited preapproach letters are not an effective way to get your foot in the door. Any reference to an individual or association removes the letter from being unsolicited, so the networking and analyzing can pay off much better than just sending what many sales organizations refer to as a letter without legs.

The Preapproach Phone Call

Making the phone follow-up to the preapproach letter is important. If you do it properly, you will get past the secretary. In larger companies, you begin the phone process with the secretary. Let's follow up on the second letter to Alice Marble. (See Figure 7–7.)

The Opening Question   The first thing you must do is ask a question. That is the way all conversations should start. The other person should get in the habit of answering your questions rather than the other way around. So find out if the person you are calling is in.

SECRETARY: "Mrs. Marble's office."

SALESPERSON: "Is she in?"

It is that simple.

F I G U R E   7–7

Preapproach Phone Call

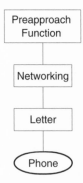

Permission to Call   Now the secretary will either say "Yes" or "No" or "Who is calling?" You should be ready with your permission to call. Start out this part of the call with your name followed by a brief summary of your letter.

"This is John Williams from Willoweed Bank. I sent Ms. Marble a letter last week. Dan Jordan at Riverside Products suggested I get in touch with her."

Now don't start blabbing! We have this tendency at this particular point to start running off rather than doing what we should be doing: Forcing some action by becoming quiet. So be quiet. Wait for the secretary to respond to your permission to call. If it's no, it is no. It doesn't mean you are inferior. It just means no. It might sound like, "I'm sorry, Ms. Marble already has strong ties with First County Savings." That's all right. It is one name that you don't put on the top of your list. But you don't throw it away either. People change and people's feelings change. If it's yes you will either talk to her at once, or she will call you back. So you should be prepared to talk once you've decided to make the call.

Introduction   Now that you have been able to get through to your prospect, you start over again. Introduce yourself and your bank and make reference to your letter.

CUSTOMER: "Hello. Alice Marble."

SALESPERSON: "Ms. Marble. This is John Williams from Willoweed Bank. Last week I sent you a letter. Dan Jordan at Riverside Products suggested I get in touch with you."

CUSTOMER: "Yes, Mr. Williams. I remember the letter. How can I help you?"

Phone Call Objective

The objective of a phone call follow-up to a preapproach letter is only to make an appointment, not to tell the prospect that the bank has 20 products and start rattling them off. Your prospect is not interested. All of your competitors have the same products. They might differ by a percentage point or two, but they are all basically the same. The phone is not the place to tell where your branches are located or anything like that. You are talking to someone who is busy. You should respect that person's time. Be brief.

"Well, I have become involved, lately, in a couple of financial alternatives for building expansions. Dan thought maybe you might be interested in talking.

"I would like the opportunity to have just an exploratory meeting with you, Ms. Marble. That way I could learn a little more about your company and you could learn about the bank."

Again, it is time to pause and listen. She will talk. You have said your piece.

Phone Call Reaction

Like the permission to call and the introduction, your prospect will either answer in the affirmative or the negative.

"Well, Mr. Williams. I appreciate your calling and I have heard many good things about Willoweed. I think for the moment we are going to hang in there with First County. We've been with them for 20 years." Or, "That might be a good idea, Mr. Williams. As you so aptly stated, this would be just an exploratory session. We have been doing business with First County for many years."

If it is negative, it is negative. Don't linger on it. Thank your prospect for her time. And, based on the previous rejection, I think I would consider that file still open but not worth pressing over the phone.

Set the Appointment

If the response is positive, then find a mutually convenient time for a meeting. Do this by offering a fairly large availability.

"Week after next, I could come out and visit with you almost any day, except, of course, Friday noon. We have a lot of your employees cashing their checks that day."

You have given her an entire week. All she needs to do is pick a slot. Suggest a brief length of time for the meeting and include your interest in seeing the operation. People who own their own businesses love to show them off.

So she might say, "Well, next Thursday in the morning looks OK."

"Perhaps, this first time, we might want to keep it to 45 minutes or so. I would like a tour of your facilities, if that would be permissible."

"I think I can arrange that. So how about 10 until 11?"

"I'm looking forward to meeting you."

Summary   In summary, the phone effort looks like this:

The Opening Question:	*SECRETARY:*	"Mrs. Marble's office."
	SALESPERSON:	"Is she in?"
Permission to call:	*SALESPERSON:*	"This is John Williams from Willoweed Bank. I sent Ms. Marble a letter last week. Dan Jordan at Riverside Products suggested I get in touch with her."
Introduction:	*CUSTOMER:*	"Hello. Alice Marble."
	SALESPERSON:	"Mrs. Marble. This is John Williams from Willoweed Bank. Last week I sent you a letter. Dan Jordan at Riverside Products suggested I get in touch with you."
	CUSTOMER:	"Yes, Mr. Williams. I remember the letter. How can I help you?"
Phone Call Objective:	*SALESPERSON:*	"Well. I have become involved, lately, in a couple of financing alternatives for building expansions. Dan thought maybe you might be interested in talking.

		"I would like the opportunity to have just an exploratory meeting with you, Ms. Marble. That way I could learn a little more about your company and you could learn about the bank."
Phone Call Reaction:	*CUSTOMER:*	"That might ba a good idea, Mr. Williams. As you so aptly stated, this would be just an exploratory session. We have been doing business with First County for many years."
Set the Appointment:	*SALESPERSON:*	"Week after next, I could come out and visit with you almost any day, except, of course, Friday noon. We have a lot of your employees cashing their checks that day."
	CUSTOMER:	"Well, next Thursday in the morning looks OK.
	SALESPERSON:	"Perhaps, this time, we might want to keep it to 45 minutes or so. I would like a tour of your facilities, if that would be permissible.
	CUSTOMER:	"I think I can arrange that. So how about 10 until 11?"
	SALESPERSON:	"I'm looking forward to meeting you."

The Introduction

The second major part of the sales model is the introduction. This entails quite a bit because it physically involves the first impression and the first words out of your mouth. When you first meet your customer, you should be totally prepared. You should have more in your attaché case than you would ever plan on leaving, just in case the prospect might ask for something other than what you had talked about.

Think carefully about how to dress for that sales call. Remember you are a banker, not a chameleon. If you call on a service station, don't feel that you need to wear dirty blue jeans. One of the distinct advantages of being a banker is to look like one. Businesses expect it; that means suits for both men and women.

The other part of greeting the customer is walking into the office, establishing eye contact, and offering a firm (not devastating) handshake. And that also means both men and women.

In Figure 7–8, showing the introductory process, you can see those functions that support greeting the customer.

The Sale

Need Analysis and Needs Fulfillment

Needs analysis and needs fulfillment are the two most important parts of selling. And although the close is included under the sale, if you are good at analyzing your customer's needs and clearly and accurately converting

F I G U R E   7–8

The Introduction

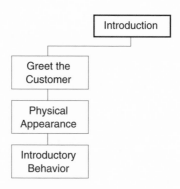

those needs into products and services, you won't really have to spend a great deal of time closing the sale. (See Figure 7–9.)

F I G U R E   7–9

The Sale

```
                        ┌─────────────┐
                        │  The Sale   │
                        └─────────────┘
        ┌──────────────────────┼──────────────────────┐
┌───────────────┐      ┌───────────────┐      ┌───────────────┐
│    Needs      │      │    Needs      │      │               │
│   Analysis    │      │  Fulfillment  │      │    Close      │
└───────────────┘      └───────────────┘      └───────────────┘
```

Chapter 6 carefully explained the process of informal questioning as well as structured questioning. Informal questioning is sales questioning (some of you might call it personal questioning). Structured questioning is product questioning. (See Figure 7–10.)

The Close

Closing is something that should happen by itself if the needs analysis and needs fulfillment are done correctly. Even so, there is still an element of driving the sale to its conclusion that involves some final sounding words.

"Here's what I think we ought to do . . ."

"So it's the receivables loan that we need to act on in conjunction with your moving your checking account over to us."

Closing is boiling down everything that you and the customer have talked about specifically into the services that the bank has to offer. These are not necessarily the bank's marketing names of the products, but the generic names for the products. Corporate banking is more realistic than retail banking. Cash management is cash management and letters of credit are letters of credit. In retail banking, many banks have Super Freddie accounts that confuse the customer rather than inform. Make sure that you refer to your products by their generic names. As part of the closing process, the salesperson begins talking about products and services more than needs and benefits. (See Figure 7–11.)

Actually, the closing process can be going along during the entire sales call through an affirmation closing process. That means that as you translate needs into products, you ask if that is the kind of approach your customer is thinking of. You are constantly seeking affirmation on the

F I G U R E   7–10

Sales Questions

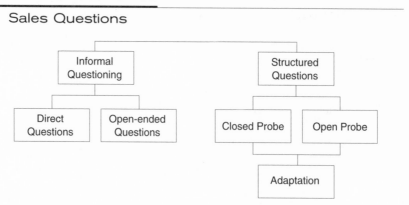

direction you are going with the sale. This technique gets the customer used to the salesperson focusing on solutions, that is, products and services.

Finally, you will want to test the waters to determine when the close should happen. You can do that with a trial closing. It is a simple question stated in a broad way. For example, "Is this the kind of thing you want to do?" Or, "Is this the direction we should be going?"

Keep your trial closings broad. Don't focus on a product. Once you focus on a product, you must be sure that the customer understands where you are going and is thoroughly ready to buy.

Finally, you may encounter rejection or objections. What if your customer says no? What if the customer disagrees? Objection and rejections should be handled the same way. Always be understanding about the objection. Don't be confrontational. Don't ask why? Instead, explain that you can see how he would feel about that particular position.

"I can see that it would be difficult to sever relations with your present bank. Especially after the last four years." Or, "Well, I can understand your concern about paying too much for financial services"

Then reflect back on the previous benefits that led the sales encounter to the point of talking about the order. "I can see that it would be difficult to sever relations with your present bank. Especially after the last four years. But you did point out to me your need for more advisory service in financing inventory. Isn't that something important to the growth of your business?" Or, "Well, I can understand your concern about paying too much for financial services, but I think as you pointed out you are going to be needing a higher level of service than before."

FIGURE 7–11

The Close

The Follow-Through

Follow-through is the last part of our sales model (see Figure 7–12). If this model were totally accurate, it would be a circle because selling and servicing in corporate banking is an ongoing process.

In terms of your routine community call program, follow-through means the thank-you letter after the sales interview. It also means a follow-up phone call. If you did not specify a time that you would get back to the prospect, you should call back in approximately 30 days. If you wait too much longer, he won't remember you. If you call too much earlier, he will think you are bugging him.

FIGURE 7–12

Follow-Through

| Preapproach Function | → | Introduction | → | The Sale | → | The Follow-Through |

| Needs Analysis | Needs Fulfillment | Close |

S U M M A R Y

1. All sales processes should operate within a specific and agreed-on model such as an effective sales model for calling on businesses.

2. The preapproach function is one part of the sales model that frequently does not appear in other sales models because it is primarily applicable to a softer sale.

3. A preapproach letter should never be more than one page.

4. The six parts to an effective phone follow-up to a preapproach letter are the opening question, permission to call, introduction, phone call objective, phone call reaction, set the appointment.

5. When you first meet your customer, you should be totally prepared. Think carefully about how to dress for that sales call. Remember you are a banker, not a chameleon.

6. Needs analysis and needs fulfillment are the two most important parts of selling.

7. When a banker closes the sale, he drives the sale to its conclusion by steering the customer along the right road.

8. Affirmation closing is when you are constantly seeking affirmation on the direction you are going with the sale.

9. Trial closing is testing the waters to determine when the close should happen.

10. Always be understanding with an objection or rejection. Agree with the customer. Explain that you can see how he feels about the particular position. Then reflect back on the previous benefits that led the sales encounter to the point of talking about the order.

11. Follow-through means the thank-you letter after the sales interview. It also means a follow-up phone call.

CHAPTER 8

Cross Selling
in the Branch

Cross selling in the branch means selling a second or third or fourth product at a sitting. Each time that customer does business in your branch, the second or third products generated from that visit are known as cross sales. That is where one draws the line between selling and order taking. Cross selling is important to you as a branch manager because you, also, must cross sell. As you will learn in Chapter 11, you must also manage your internal selling effort. It is very difficult to manage a process with which you are unfamiliar.

Review the following controversial situation: Mrs. Arnold walks into my branch. She approaches me. I stand up and greet her. Motioning to the chair in front of my desk, I ask her what we can do for her. She responds that she would like to open a checking account. I open it for her. She is happy. I wish her a happy day. She leaves—happy.

Is that a sale? No. That is called LUCK! Many people disagree. Many people refer to that situation as having sold a checking account. In actuality that checking account has nothing to do with selling. That is order taking—plain and simple. It is no different than walking into a diner and ordering a cheeseburger. The waitress in the diner certainly doesn't consider herself a salesperson or the order as a sale.

Order taking requires good customer-service skills: Establishing eye contact with the customer. Standing when they approach your desk.

Referring to them by name. Thanking them at the end of the transaction. This is customer service, not sales.

CONVINCING SELLING

Let's look at another situation: A customer comes into your branch. You are busy as are your customer service reps. You decide that you will have to handle this customer. She is standing in the lobby looking around as if someone had just dropped her in the middle of someone else's living room, perplexed in wonderment.

"Good morning," you say in a pleasant way. "May I help you?"

"Yes. I didn't realize how busy this branch is. Is it always this way?" she asks, making a sweeping motion with her arm.

"Well, Fridays are very busy here. Mostly people cashing their pay-checks or needing some additional service. Would you care to have a seat in my office?"

"Yes. That would be nice." she states, as the two of you walk into your office and you motion for her to sit down.

"I'm Jack Drew. I manage this branch. What can we do for you?"

"Well, Mr. Drew," she begins. "I need to find out about your check-ing accounts. You see my husband and I just moved here from Sioux Falls."

Then you go through your litany of advantages for your product. She counters with what she used to have. You counter with what your particular marketing area offers. She counters with what your competition has. You counter with why your bank is better. Finally, she agrees and opens a checking account. It took eight minutes. Is that a sale?

Many bank executives believe that is the basis for selling and teach-ing people how to sell. Those banks support that kind of a situation as the premise for building a sales culture.

I contend that kind of a situation is not really selling but more a part of marketing and merchandising.

"But," you sputter, "I had to convince her to use my bank." I agree. I also know that your bank has probably spent a lot of money getting that customer into your branch through advertising, branch location, decor, point of sale, and brochures. Your primary job in this situation is to be the tail end of a marketing effort. That is called convincing selling. As you look at Figure 8–1, note that convincing selling is part of the internal selling function. Cross selling is the other type of internal selling. In the figure, you can see how selling can be categorized within a branch banking environ-

F I G U R E   8–1

Types of Branch Selling: Convincing Selling

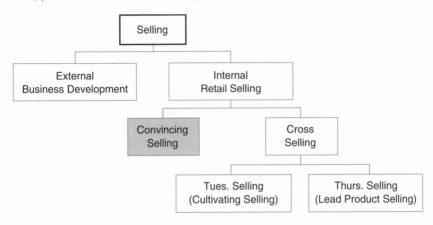

ment. As you will learn in Chapter 11, this categorizing is important to measure sales performance accurately. Even though there is cross selling in all departments within a bank, the most controversial type of cross selling inside the branches is done by the customer service personnel.

The second situation with Jack Drew and the customer from Sioux Falls is a good example of convincing selling. That is when the customer service personnel truly have to internalize the needs of the customer and satisfy those needs with a banking product and service. Convincing selling takes some hard thinking and utilizes all of the traditional selling skills. So, in that sense, it is selling. That is the kind of selling we are expected to do, anyway. CSRs all tell me that is what they are being paid for.

As a manager, it is impossible to determine the difference between the first situation that we call luck and the second situation that we call convincing selling. Although those situations are difficult for managers to differentiate, cross selling is easy to spot and easy to measure. Cross selling is selling related products off a lead product.

LEAD PRODUCTS

If you go to McDonalds and ask for a cheeseburger, the counter person will ask you if you would like french fries. (For that matter, if you ask for ice cream, the counter person will ask if you want french fries!) If you buy a suit, the salesperson will ask you if you would like to see some blouses, shirts, and ties. All cross selling is based on a thorough understanding of the lead products—the suit, the cheeseburger. I have taught sporting goods retailers to pinpoint lead products. For example, a tennis racquet is a lead product. From that lead product flows a variety of related cross sales: string, racquet case, extra racquet grip, balancing lead, and the inevitable tennis balls. The string, racquet case, grip, and lead are the real related products. Tennis balls are more often a lead product than a cross sell.

The astute sporting goods retailer would provide a lead product sales path to his sales team that would look like that shown in Figure 8–2. The first step for the retailer is to determine his lead products. What are the top products that customers ask for? Those are lead products.

We have lead products in retail banking. They are checking, savings, CDs, and loans. Those four products account for slightly more than 85 percent of the products customers ask for; the rest (more than 20 products) account for 15 percent.

Most branches are different, otherwise we could say that all branches did 25 percent checking, 25 percent savings, 25 percent CDs, and 10 percent loans. In actuality, that is the way it averages out for customer service (platform) personnel. I have sold in branches where CDs account for 60 percent and savings accounts for 30 percent. Those branches are inundated by the blue-haired army. That is an entirely different kind of sale. In other branches, checking is 60 percent, savings 5 percent, CDs 15 percent, and loans 20 percent. Those branches are the yuppies; they have highly transient, quick business. Run!

F I G U R E   8–2

Lead Product Sales Path (Sporting Goods)

Tennis Racquet

String

Grip Over-wrap

Balancing Lead

As a good branch manager, you need to know the market. If it is mixed, what are your percentages? Fill out the relative weights of the lead products for your branch in Figure 8–3. You might want to have your customer service personnel tell you what they think the percentages are. Then you can average them. Once you can compile your branch's lead products, you have an overview of the account activity in your branch and cross selling becomes much more predictable.

I will never forget the first time that I sat at a desk and sold. I was scared to death! The thought of having to memorize all of the products that the bank had to offer was overpowering. I memorized Individual Retirement Accounts, Guaranteed Student Loans/Parent Loans, Sweep Accounts, Discount Brokerage, and on and on. My wife diligently grilled me on the details:

"If you are married and have no 401K at work, how much can you and your wife put aside tax-free?"

"Uhh," I chewed on my knuckles, "$2,200 each."

"Now what about for the dog?"

"Dog? I didn't read that. How much?" I was panicking.

"Take it easy. Dogs are not included."

"Whew," I sighed, thumbing through more of my notes.

Then I went in for my first day. I got there early, organized my desk, and double-checked where I kept all of my brochures and account opening documents. Then the customers came in. The first one asked me for a checking account. Hot dog! I thought. I know this one backwards and forwards. I rattled off the features of those accounts so fast my customer didn't know what I was talking about. She left. I sold a checking account, I thought.

My next customer came in. A gentleman asked for a checking account. Same thing. Boy, am I lucky, I thought.

Next customer: Checking account. Didn't buy. Just fishing.

Next customer: CD. I was ready. $5,000. Six months. Easy stuff!

F I G U R E   8–3

Your Branch's Lead Products

Ck		Sav		CD		Loans		Other	
%	+	%	+	%	+	%	+	%	= 100%

Next customer: Checking account. Cut and paste!

Next customer: Car loan. A little variety.

Last customer of the day: Checking.

After three weeks of this (the busiest branch of a bank in Long Island), I had opened 81 accounts: 56 checking accounts, 18 loan applications, and 7 CDs. That was a lot. Then I wondered, what about discount brokerage? And I remembered that no one asked me about the Cirrus Network for ATMs.

In banking we open only about three or four accounts (checking, savings, and CDs) and we cross sell off of those basic lead products. That's what cross selling is all about. When you look at it from a simplistic point of view, it becomes very easy. Effective cross selling requires that you know your lead products and related products. Write them down and have them in front of you. Customers don't object.

For example, if a customer asks me for a checking account, I have a small CRT screen in the back of my head that magically lights up. It shows me the products related to that checking account in the order that I would sell them. My mental CRT screen looks like Figure 8–4.

F I G U R E   8–4

Cross Selling a Checking Account

CHECKING

ATM

DD

SAV

OD

REALISTIC SUCCESS RATIOS FOR A REALISTIC SALES PATH

I have done the checking account path so many times that I know the success percentage from taking an order for checking to selling ATM (92 percentage). I cross sold direct deposits, using forms that the customer signs and the bank mails to the employer (89 percent). I cross sold overdraft as a feature on our checking in the event of an accidental overdraft (71 percent). I suggested a savings program linking their checking with the ATM card (47 percent).

When you cross sell day after day, you begin to put together your own system.

The chart in Figure 8–5 illustrates a lead product sales path for six frequently asked for lead products. (Individual retirement accounts [IRAs] are generally seasonal lead products in the spring.)

Notice that internal branch cross selling consists of 6 lead products from which 11 total products are sold. So a CSR intent on working smart versus working hard learns 11 products backwards and forwards:

Checking accounts	Automatic teller machine cards
Savings accounts	Direct deposit
Certificates of deposit	Overdraft protection
Individual retirement accounts	Equity credit lines
Money market accounts	Automatic loan payments
Installment loans	

The most frequently used sales paths are (1) checking > ATM > direct deposit > overdraft protection > savings and (2) certificates of deposit > savings or checking > ATM > equity credit line. Those two make up approximately 65 percent of your cross-selling time. Looked at another way, those two paths apply to every other customer! That means learning seven products really well. Now how does one go about cross selling those products? You can try it this way:

BANKER: "Good morning. May I help you?"

CUSTOMER: "Yes. I'm in a rush. I need to open your basic checking account. I know all about it. Here is a money order for $1,000. It will only be my name on the signature cards."

BANKER: "Well, that should be easy. Just sign here and here."

CUSTOMER: "Great. Thank you very much."

F I G U R E   8–5

Lead Product Sales Path

Lead Product	CHKING ATM	SVNGS ATM	CD	IRA	MMDA	LOAN
	⬇	⬇	⬇	⬇	⬇	⬇
	DD	DD	SAV (or CK)	DD	CK	AUTO PYMT
Sales Path	⬇	⬇	⬇	⬇	⬇	⬇
	SAV	CK	CK/ATM or (SAV/ATM)	CK	IRA	CK
	⬇	⬇	⬇	⬇	⬇	⬇
	OD	OD	ECL	SAV	SAV	ATM

Key:
CK = Checking, DD = Direct Deposit, ECL = Equity Credit Line, OD = Overdraft Protection

BANKER: "How about an ATM card?"

CUSTOMER: "I don't think so. Not now."

BANKER: "How about direct deposit for your paycheck?"

CUSTOMER: "Nahh. That's too complicated."

BANKER: "How about a savings account? We've got some great ones!"

CUSTOMER: "Not today. I'm in a rush."

BANKER: "OK. Have a nice day."

That is "how 'bout a" selling. This high-risk selling works sometimes. You will get a lot of nos. So if you get flustered by rejections, I would strongly suggest that you don't do how 'bout a. Unfortunately, when you push how 'bout a selling, the customer is uneasy. The image of the bank becomes tarnished. Even such evasive maneuvers as, "Can I interest you in our savings accounts?" is still how 'bout a. The underlying problem in this situation is that the sales momentum is hindered because the banker is asking questions without regard to the customer's needs. "How about a checking account?" What if the customer doesn't need one? You should ask brief qualifying questions that allow you to decide the kind of product mix the customer should have.

If you and your staff have not predetermined what those questions are, your staff probably will not be successful in cross selling.

QUALIFYING QUESTIONS

Several years ago after I finished conducting a two-day sales training seminar, a customer service representative came up. I was sure she was going to tell me what a great job I had done.

"I've been to a lot of sales training seminars," she began.

"No kidding. How'd I do?"

"About the same as everyone else. You're just funnier."

That was like being hit between the eyes with a line drive. I didn't know what to say.

"Please don't take that the wrong way," she continued. It's just that theory is theory. I have heard it all. I need to figure out how to do it."

I squinched up my forehead in a puzzled expression. "How to do it?" I repeated.

"Yeah. For example, what do I say?"

"What do you mean, what do you say?"

"When a customer walks up to me and asks for a checking account, what do I say?"

I was stunned. "Uhh," I intelligently continued, "you mean you want me to tell you the words?"

"Exactly. What do I say?"

I had to confess that I didn't know. The following week, I put my entire company on alert that we needed to go to our member banks and become internal salespeople. Our mission was to learn the words. Ever since then, all of the key managers and trainers in my company have to spend one day each month inside a bank cross selling and analyzing the words.

The words are questions. I have tried a variety of questions with which to answer my customer's first question. My questions parallel the sales path.

For example, a customer approaches my desk. I stand up and greet the customer and offer him a seat.

"I'd like some information on your checking accounts."

"Have you ever had a checking account?" I ask.

"Well, uh. Yes. I have one now. We're moving into this area."

"Did your checking account have a minimum balance?" I continue.

"It certainly did. $500," my customer responds.

"Was that easy for you to maintain?"

"Yeah. We never had a problem with it."

"Do you write a lot of checks?"

"Just the ordinary house bills and cash. Yeah. Probably 10 to 15."

"Well," I continue, "our checking account requires only a $400 minimum balance. You can write as many checks as you want and we'll pay you 5.25 percent on the unused balance. Is that the kind of account you'd be interested in?"

"That sounds great."

"Wonderful. Just sign here . . . and here."

"What's this for?" the customer asks, referring to the ATM application.

"That's for your ATM card. It's standard equipment on your checking account. And its free, as long as you use it in one of our locations."

"That's the way my present one works."

Noticing the customer's name on the signature card, I say, "Mr. Smith, do you work locally?"

"I will be, as soon as I'm transferred. At IBM."

"We have a direct deposit relationship with them. All that means is that you don't have to stand in one of those lines," I say, pointing to the queue winding around the lobby. "Unless you would prefer to."

"Gaad no. That's a good idea," he states happily.

"If you'll just sign this direct deposit form, we'll send it to IBM, and they will automatically deposit your paycheck in your checking account."

"Sounds great. I appreciate that."

"I know you're in a rush, but our checking account features a very helpful safety function. It covers any accidental overdraft that might occur on your account . . . like my wife and I sometimes forget to make note of all our ATM withdrawals, and if the month is tight, we might create an accidental overdraft. You only pay for it when you use it, otherwise it's free."

"That's not a bad idea. I'm on the road so much and we both have ATM cards."

"One last service to make your banking relationship more convenient; with your checking account and ATM card, you can move money from your checking account to a savings account, again without incurring the wait in those lines. It's all very easy. We link your checking to your savings. The ATM machine tells you what to do. It's a great way to save for your vacation."

"But I don't have a savings account."

"Well. That's not a problem. I'll be happy to open one for you."

Checking > ATM > direct deposit > overdraft > savings. A simple, direct sales path developed through qualifying questions (the words). Let's examine those questions.

1. Banker's checking account inquiry: "Have you ever had one before?"
2. Banker's qualifying questions for checking account:
   a. "How much of a minimum balance are you used to keeping?"
   b. "How many checks do you write?"
3. Banker's qualifying statement for ATM: "Sign here . . . and here."
4. Banker's qualifying questions for direct deposit "Do you work locally?"
5. Banker's qualifying statement for overdraft protection: "Our checking account features a very helpful safety function that covers any accidental overdraft."
6. Banker's qualifying statement for savings: "We link your checking to your savings."

Seven qualifying statements and questions resulted in one first account and four sales (or second accounts). Research shows that the average bank can open a checking account in five minutes operationally. The cross sales take another four. Nine minutes for five accounts! Time yourself.

It is a well-known fact in the financial services industry that customer service personnel in banks (including branch manager) do not attempt to get the second accounts for one reason or another. Maybe the CSRs just don't know the right words. Worse yet, maybe the branch manager doesn't know the words.

The sales path I just described isn't necessarily the only one. Some banks prefer not to introduce the direct deposit service because they rely on the customer to instigate that. So those banks might do checking > ATM > telephone transfer > savings, or a version of that. The important thing, from the manager's point of view, is that every person in your branch who has the responsibility of opening new accounts should have six sales paths written down in front of them. With those sales paths should be the introductory words.

When I sell in a branch, the first thing I try to find out are the percentages of checking, savings, and CDs that are first accounts. Then I write down three sales paths with the words.

Figure 8–6 contains my checking sales starter.

Cross selling is the process of thinking in terms of related products and then figuring out how to qualify a customer to make sure she needs one. You should be sensitive to the fact that you are providing products and services that your customer needs. It's like the two gears in Chapter 5 (page 59), one gear is customer needs and the other is banking services. A sale occurs when those two gears mesh. I don't want you to think that all cross selling is simply turning on your mental CRT and building sales paths so that you can rattle off services. The actual sales path can be used effectively in Thursday selling and Tuesday selling.

Let's look at the sales types diagram in Figure 8–7. Thursday selling occurs when your branch is busy (incidentally, this is not a good day

F I G U R E   8–6

Checking Sales Starter

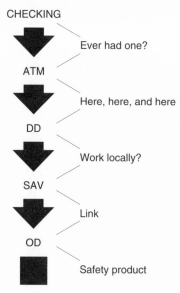

FIGURE 8-7

Types of Branch Selling: Cross Selling

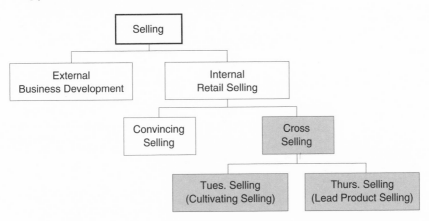

to do external selling). You can use the sales path and words very effectively on busy days.

Tuesday selling occurs when the branch isn't as busy. You can take more time to cultivate relationships with your customers. You can spend more time finding out what their personal financial needs are, so you can realistically address how the bank can be of assistance. Yet you still need that CRT screen in your head and you still need the words as starters. With Tuesday selling, you can ask more open-ended questions and spend more time listening.

Even convincing selling needs a sales path and the words. If you need to take the time to convince a customer to invest money in your CD, you might as well spend a few more minutes cross selling those products that will allow that CD to be an effective investment vehicle. It's only fair to the customer.

SUMMARY

1. Cross selling in the branch means selling a second or third or fourth product at a sitting. It is selling related products off a lead product.

2. Checking, savings, CDs, and loans are the lead products in retail banking.

3. The basic selling types in retail banking are external business development and internal retail selling, which is composed of convincing selling and cross selling (Tuesday and Thursday selling.)

4. The most frequently used sales paths are (1) checking > ATM > direct deposit > overdraft protection> savings and (2) certificates of deposit > savings or checking > ATM > equity credit line.

5. The words are questions that internal bank salespeople use to guide the cross-sales process. They parallel the sales path.

CHAPTER 9

Finding and Building Better Product Knowledge

Product knowledge is a very important part of selling. I am sure you have heard that so many times that repetition at this point could produce boredom! In retail banking, however, the bank's internal system focuses on retail services and products. As a branch manager, your management is now telling you to sell the bank's products and services to small businesses, as well as walk-in consumers. The problems associated with accepting the responsibility of small business sales is fully understanding the needs of the small business owner and the products/services that satisfy those needs. Many bank executives today believe it is your job to learn those products and services yourself.

You can look at business development product knowledge in two ways: First, learning about the actual products and services of the bank that small business persons need to effectively operate their business. Second, learning about the products and services of the bank that small business employees need to effectively operate their homes. Both of these kinds of products and services should be the realm of the astute retail business development officer.

BUSINESS PRODUCTS AND SERVICES

Because of the many products and services related to financial institutions, being an authority on all of them is very difficult. For example, if you are involved in commercial lending or trust services for a major global bank, you would get heavily involved in cash management services such as account reconcilement, automated balance reporting, lock box, zero-balance accounts, and more. The major banks are carving out a specific niche for themselves so they can focus on specific products for a specific community business market.

Where and How to Find Product Information

There are many ways to learn about the products and their usage by businesses. Bankers have access to information about financial products. They can attend seminars. Local bank associations hold product seminars quite often. Some of these seminars are introductory and provide a basic understanding of business products and services. Another source of learning is casual discussions with other managers or especially with members of the corporate or commercial group within your bank.

Many banks request that the corporate groups hold ongoing product seminars for the branches so they can learn more about those business products that help the small business person to operate more profitably. When developing your calling territory, you might want to make calls with a member of the corporate staff to better internalize exactly what the needs of the small business person are.

You can also gain product knowledge from financial institutions, literature, associations, advertisements, books about the small business person, and at times through service catalogs. A word of warning about service catalogs is that they have historically been developed as reference materials, not as sales aids. Consequently, the information is extremely features oriented. If a service catalog is any good, there should be explanations of products and their relationships to each other. The real value of today's banking is the grouping of products to satisfy myriad customer needs.

Many banks are replacing the traditional service catalog with individual product profiles that explain product features, product benefits, and related products.

Banking Products and Services Used by Small Businesses

As a retail banker who is expanding into the business community, you should focus on specific products that allow you to get your foot in the door. Financial products and services for the small business can be grouped into three categories:

1. Primary business services
2. Money management services
3. Trust services

Primary Business Services

Primary business services include business checking vehicles, business credit card vehicles, automatic deposits, and loans. Businesses have to write checks to pay vendors. They have to have places to deposit the money they receive for their products. They need checking vehicles of some sort. A checking relationship is a very basic level of banking relationship. It is your foot in the door, the most needed account for any business. Research shows us that small business owners generally establish a banking relationship with the closest or first bank they meet. There is little shopping around. There is little loyalty as well. Small business owners easily move their checking accounts if there is something in it for them.

Small business owners start their banking relationships with some kind of a checking account. It could be a regular business checking account with monthly maintenance fees and per-check charges or some kind of sweep account that takes money (over a stated amount) and puts it in an interest-bearing account.

Most small businesses use their banks for checking and credit card services. From time to time as they attempt to grow, they evolve into a lending relationship. That relationship will not necessarily be with the bank they started with.

In your dealings with small businesses, you should visualize a staged small business sales path. It would start with an elementary group of related products, as shown in Figure 9–1. When you make business calls, have these related products in mind. However, keep your mind open to other products and services that the business prospect needs. And like developing the words in retail selling, you need to develop words in external selling; questions that reveal needs: Which banks do they presently have their business checking accounts with? Are they happy with their present banks? And so on. In your mind, ask questions that follow a sales path. Your prospect will either follow that path, or together you will create an alternate one.

F I G U R E   9–1

Small Business Sales Path

Business Checking

Credit Card Services

Night Drop

Federal Tax Deposits

My primary sales path starts with a checking account. For a retail establishment, I know that most will need some kind of credit card affiliation. I shy away from the telephone call-in-your-account-number-type of credit card, mainly because there is so much fraud in the credit card business. A tangible location with real customers walking through the door allows the retailer and the banker less chance of fraud.

With my credit card sale, I am ensuring larger deposits into my customer's business checking account. If my customer wants a terminal she would need to rent this from the bank. Otherwise my customer would buy an imprinter.

I would provide a night drop for the retailer and his federal tax deposits. That is a good conservative path for you to visualize as you call on retailers. It can be embellished to include lending as depicted in Figure 9–2.

As an astute business banker, make sure that the retailer's employees can avoid lines and have their payroll checks automatically deposited into your bank. That is just sound business banking. At that point you will have a firm, well-grounded relationship with your retailer. As long as you service that account well, it will not move to another bank.

As part of your servicing job, you should listen carefully to your client, anticipating some kind of lending activity. That could range from lending based on receivables, to lending based on inventory, to lending secured by business real estate, to lending secured personally by real estate. As you learn in the following chapter, expansion and growth

F I G U R E   9–2

Small Business Sales Path

Business Checking

Credit Card Services

Night Drop

Federal Tax Deposits

Direct Deposit

Loans

invariably lead to real estate because real estate can be used by the owner to house the business as well as to provide an investment for later return.

Another sales path that I pursue from time to time is shown in Figure 9–3. The King's Kamera case study in the following chapter allows you to see how this sales path could happen. Some retailers carry large balances in their checking accounts; but not because they want to. In many cases, they are not even aware that they do carry large balances. Most small businesses start out with a standard business checking account, they don't necessarily upgrade their banking services as they become financially successful. Owners have a lot of things on their mind. They are trying to run a business. It takes a clever banker to help the retailer make more money. That is the best benefit in the world. When you can function as another source of income for your customer rather than a series of charges and fees, your customer will begin utilizing your bank's services.

Some banks offer sweep accounts that automatically sweep month-end excess money. Otherwise you have to ask them to periodically check their balances. When the balance exceeds a certain number, the owner can

F I G U R E   9–3

Small Business Sales Path

Business Checking

Telephone Transfer

Money Market Account

Corporate Credit Card

do a telephone transfer into a money market account or a certificate of deposit. In general, I find that small businesses are always struggling with cash flow and prefer not to have their money tied up in a certificate. They prefer a money market account.

Finally, customers who appear to have excess cash from time to time could effectively manage a corporate credit card. A sweep account or checking, telephone transfer, money market arrangement is a signal to build a rationale for a corporate credit card. You should become aware of current IRS rulings in regard to corporate credit cards. In many cases, it is better to have personal credit cards whose legitimate business expenses are reimbursable by the company.

Banks, depending on the market niche they are carving, organize their sales emphasis in many different ways. Some will tell their branch managers not to do business development. They put commercial loan officers in small regional clusters. Some set specific business call targets for their branch managers. Some use their branch managers as mortgage originators backed up with a small staff of inhouse account executives to support that effort.

If your bank is concentrating on the mortgage market and has asked you to make calls into this market, you have an opportunity to create new business relationships in addition to the mortgage business for the bank. Most of the mortgage business you get for the bank will come from Realtors®. You will be spending your time romancing Realtors. Many bankers forget that Realtors are businesses that also need banking products and services. Quite simply, the sales path in Figure 9–4 lists the mortgage you will generate through a Realtor and the related small business banking products the Realtor would use.

Money Management Services

The second group of small business products or services is money management services. These include those products and services that profitable businesses or high-income individuals within a profitable family business should use as safe investment vehicles. I separate this from trust services even though in many banks they are grouped together.

Certificates, Treasury Vehicles, Municipals, and Mutual Funds
In Figure 9–5 we illustrate the products in a grid. Some of the fixed elements of the grid are filled in. You are to fill in those variable elements.

Trust Services

The third products and services group is trust. Again, this is an area that should be referred to a trust specialist. Clients of yours who have recent-

FIGURE 9–4

Sales Path for Realtors

Mortgage

Business Checking

Telephone Transfer

Money Market Account

Corporate Credit Card

FIGURE 9-5

Money Management Service Products

Security	Minimum Purchase Term	Taxable Liability	Safety	Liquidity	Fees	Payment of Interest
Certificate of deposit	14 days or longer	Fully taxable	FDIC coverage up to $100 M	Subject to early w/d penalty		At maturity semiannual 18 mos. or +
Repurchase agreement	3–89 days	Fully taxable	Secured by collateral of bank's portfolio	Subject to collateral inventory		At maturity
Savings certificates	3–6 months	Fully taxable	FDIC coverage up to $100 M	Subject to early w/d penalty		At maturity
Savings certificates	1–5 years	Fully taxable	FDIC coverage up to $100 M	Subject to early w/d penalty		At maturity
Municipal notes and bonds	1–20 years	Fully exempt in state issued	Credit of issuing municipality	Sold at market price		Semiannual
Commercial paper	3–279 days	Fully taxable	Unsecured debt of issuing company	Must hold to maturity		At maturity
Treasury bills	3 months to 1 year	State tax exempt	Primary obligation of U.S. govt.	Sold at market price		Purchased at discount matures at par
Treasury notes	2–10 years	State tax exempt	Primary obligation of U.S. govt.	Sold at market price		Semiannual
Treasury bonds	10–30 years	State tax exempt	Primary obligation of U.S. govt.	Sold at market price		Semiannual
Agency notes	6 months to 10 years	State tax exempt	Secondary obligation of U.S. govt.	Sold at market price		Semiannual
Mutual funds	2 years or longer	As specified by portfolio		Sold at NAV		Monthly or have compounded

ly sold their businesses, come into an inheritance, won a lottery, had a successful lawsuit, or who have retired could avail themselves of a strong relationship with the trust department of your bank. Products and services in this realm are

1. Personal trust services (custody, investment advisory, living trust).
2. Trust/investment management (savings/CDs, all personal trust services).

An effective exercise is to develop a product analysis form on each of the primary business banking products. Simply going through the exercise of filling in this form will give you insight into the usage of the product or service and competitive factors of the product or service. You might want to make up a form similar to Figure 9–6 for each primary product (see page 132).

Many of your business customers will need other services that the bank has to offer. These services might very well be unfamiliar to you. As a community business development banker, you should not be expected to be an authority on corporate, trust, or money management services. Even such products as repurchase agreements; municipal notes and bonds; commercial paper; Treasury bills, notes, and bonds; and agency notes are all financial products that require a specialist. In addition, the terms change, the fees change, and the minimum purchase changes from time to time.

As part of your product knowledge growth process, you need to know the names of those individuals within the bank who can provide you with general information and then back up that information with a joint sales call with you. You should have the names of individuals in corporate banking, trust services, and money management.

S U M M A R Y

1. Business development product knowledge has two parts: First, the actual products and services of the bank that small business persons need to order to effectively operate their businesses. And, second, the products and services of the bank that small business employees need to operate their homes.
2. Financial products and services for the small business can be grouped into three categories: Primary business services, money management services, trust services.

3. A retail banker should focus on those specific products that will allow her to get a foot in the door: business checking vehicles, credit card vehicles, automatic deposits, and loans.

4. At the beginning of a sales call, create a mental sales path, assume your customer will either follow that path or together you will create an alternate one.

FIGURE 9–6

Primary Product Sales Information

Name of product _____   Date _____

Features of product   Benefits of the product

_____   _____

_____   _____

_____   _____

Name of competition's product _____

Features of competition's product   Benefits of the product

_____   _____

_____   _____

_____   _____

Name of competition's product _____

Features of competition's product   Benefits of the product

_____   _____

_____   _____

_____   _____

Objections to using the product (too expensive, too much trouble, already have it)

_____

_____

_____

Good leading questions _____

_____

_____

_____

Helping Small Businesses Make Money

This chapter about how businesses make money is written for the average branch manager. It might dip into some corporate (or commercial) banking products, but in general it is information for a community banking manager.

I have been a small businessman for 25 years. I have friends who have small businesses. We talk a lot. We talk about bankers a lot. They know that I deal with bankers. My friends have noticed that a lot more bankers are calling on them than five (or even two) years ago. One said recently, "You know, up until a couple of years ago, I never had a banker call me. That would have been absurd. I never even expected it. But now I probably get calls from two or three different banks a year. And I'm small potatoes, just another fitness center in a town where there's already three."

Bankers making sales calls on smaller businesses in a community are not the commercial lenders, who call on bigger customers or heavy borrowers. Smaller community banks might have a commercial division with two or three loan officers. They should be called on to assist the branch manager rather than replace him.

I have noticed that most branch managers—for that matter, most bankers—don't know how their customers make money. I have heard bankers tell me that is not their business. They believe their business is to provide the financial products or services—not to provide financial and management consulting. That mentality keeps small bankers comfortably situated in their offices. The aggressive, innovative banker realizes she must pass along the immense amount of information regarding products to the bank's business customers. That doesn't mean to pass along the features of products; most customers don't care about the features. Customers are interested in what the product or service is going to do to help them make more money.

Businesses are in business to make money. I tell you that as a business owner, I am here to make money. My friend who owns King's Kamera is there to make money. The owner of Lee Advertising is in business to make as much money as she can so some innovative investor will come along and buy her out. You will meet both Mike King and Marilee Lewis (Lee Advertising) later in this chapter. You will also learn relevant concerns of different businesses and which hot buttons to push.

Let me say again that businesses are in business to make money. They are not in business to open checking accounts. You will not endear yourself to customers by suggesting that they open business checking accounts with your bank. They couldn't care less! They need to know why—what's in it for them? The small business owner is more bottom-line oriented than a large business manager because the small business owner has personal holdings at stake. That is an important thing to remember. Most small business owners who have attempted to grow or survive have had to risk their homes or personal savings. That makes them a different kind of animal than a business school MBA who manages a product line for General Motors Corporation.

When the risk affects your family, you learn to become innovative, imaginative, and hardworking or you end up working for someone who is willing to risk at that level. As a small business owner, you live for the day that you don't have to incur personal risk. Wouldn't it be great to borrow $100,000 without putting up your house as collateral?

As a branch manager, you will be speaking with business owners. You will work with a lot of family businesses. You will learn that most family businesses are run by people who feel guilty that they have sacrificed their family for the business. They want to talk about their family as much as their business. And therein lies the secret to a banker's success in doing business with the small business person.

Learn about the business and learn about the family. If the business is going to be a client of the bank, the bank will probably want collateral from the family. A good salesperson keeps a very up-to-date file on the small business customer. Here's a fairly corny song I once heard. It's entitled "Sales Information":

> The business owner. The owner's spouse.
> The owner's children. The owner's house.
> The owner's hobbies. The owner's pets.
> The favorite ties and favored blouse.

I take this song seriously; I have memorized it. (I don't tell most people that, only my readers.) When I call on customers, before I leave the sales interview, as a review process in my mind, I recite, owner, spouse, children, house, hobbies, pets, ties, and blouse. Actually, the lyrics apply to any sales prospect. It is just that business owners seem to be more conscious of family since they risk it from day to day.

Recently, I was in New York City calling on a major international law firm with the president of the New York office of an international banking firm. We met with a French attorney and talked about their non-U.S. clients who were interested in starting offshore corporations to minimize tax vulnerability. It was a product sales call from beginning to end. I was waiting for the conversation to shift to find out about the attorney. In my mind, I kept reciting, owner, spouse, children, house, hobbies, pets, ties, and blouse.

Finally, just before we were ready to leave, I asked, "Just out of curiosity, Marcel, how did you ever get involved in a U.S. law firm?" That was the beginning of a long conversation revealing information on his parents, triple citizenship, and restaurant preferences. When I left, I knew that I had adequate information on Marcel so that the next time I picked up the phone to call him, I would have something with which to start the conversation.

Here's an example: "Marcel, Dwight Ritter, here. I was talking with a guy in Luxembourg last week with a double citizenship and told him I knew someone with three citizenships."

"Hello, Dwight. What were his two citizenships?"

"Born in Hong Kong to Belgium parents."

"Looks like he won't need a passport." And the conversation would continue from there, evolving into the business at hand. If I didn't know anything about Marcel, the next conversation would be very formal, perhaps slightly uncomfortable.

As a perceptive banker and salesperson, realize that part of your sales exploration must include those personal things the owner likes to talk about.

Let me simplify the process of running a business by stating that businesses make money in two ways: by decreasing expenses and/or increasing sales. That's what business is all about, bringing money in and spending as little as possible (so the owner can put more in her pocket).

The older a business is, the greater the chance that time alone has added expenses an owner cannot see. For example, I have a friend in the mortuary business. It is a three-generation business. His father hired one person to do the bookkeeping 20 years ago. He also hired an office manager. Today, the son does not need a bookkeeper and office manager. Due to advances in computer accounting software and word processing, he only needs one person. But, both people are part of the family. What do you do, especially since other expenses have gone up disproportionately? He has elected not to invest in a $400 accounting software program until Muriel ($21,000/year) retires, which is three years away. And since I run my own business, and have for 25 years, I can understand that. As a matter of fact, I would bet that my friend will probably take less home, personally, to keep Muriel on the payroll. An established two- to three-generation family business is probably riddled with expenses that are unnecessary. Some are personnel expenses the owner will elect to live with. Other expenses might be controllable.

On the other side from expenses is income—money coming in. Here businesses really vary from the small one-person consulting operation that charges an hourly rate to a bank that charges fees and interest. The one-person consulting operation brings in, say, $1,000. That $1,000 represents about 90 percent income to the consultant. He pays very few direct business expenses to earn that fee. The banker brings in a deposit of $1,000. That $1,000 doesn't even belong to the bank until it can loan it out and earn some money on it. If the banker does a good job, the bank might earn 1 percent on that money.

All of the businesses you will encounter fall between 90 percent and 1 percent. And all of those businesses will be obsessed with controlling expenses and increasing sales. As an effective banker, you must learn to refocus your role. You should not see yourself as just another supplier when, in actuality, you are a financial advisor (as far as most companies are concerned). You are the one who knows about money. You should be able to do more than sell a business checking account.

HOW YOU KNOW IF SOMEONE IS MAKING MONEY

A sale is a sale is a sale. Every sales dollar has three parts to it: First is the *income* from the sale. Second is how much the seller paid for the product that he sold. That's called the *cost of goods sold.* Third is the total amount of money the seller spent actually running the business. That's called *operating expense.* Now add the cost of goods sold plus operating expense and if they are less than the number of dollars received from customers (income), then the seller made some money.

Most companies are concerned about the difference between income and cost of goods sold plus operating expense—their margin. Basically, *a margin is what you get when you divide the gross profit by the net sales.*

Let's assume you own a retail business. You sell sporting goods. Last year, you received $500,000 from a customer who bought your sporting goods. You bought those sporting goods from a manufacturer for $390,000. That means you had a gross profit of $110,000 and a gross margin of 22 percent.

$$\text{Gross margin} = \frac{\text{Gross profit}}{\text{Net sales}}$$

In most retail businesses, margins are around 15 to 30 percent, depending on the specific industry.

When you talk to a prospective customer, she might tell of really being strangled because the margin is only 20 percent. Don't be too alarmed until you find out what the industry average is. You can do that easily by contacting the retail industry's national association. Almost every retail industry has an association that reports average margins from its membership. That is very helpful to new owners. It is also very helpful to an innovative banker. The problem is that as a banker, you will find it very difficult to get the associations to give you any information unless you join the association.

During your first visit to a prospective retail customer, a good question would be, "Is a 15 percent margin fairly standard in your industry?" Even though you don't know what is standard in the industry, you do know that most retail industries are going to be near 15 percent. They will let you know.

You shouldn't have to commit to memory a dozen margins; instead use a chart similar to Figure 10–1. Actually, aggressive branch managers find out margins for only those retail businesses that look promising in their area.

F I G U R E   10–1

Industry Average Figures

Business	Gross Margin	Square Feet	Number of Employees
Pharmacy			
Gift store			
Sporting goods store			
Camera store			
Restaurant			
Fast-food restaurant			
Hardware store			
Advertising agency			
Small manufacturer			

Beyond the obvious dollars and sense of analyzing the ability of a small business to make money, there are a few nonfinancial indicators you should look at.

Knowledgeable Management

An important aspect of running a business is having a smart manager. Business managers who have enrolled in some local executive development programs are prone to be more solid and less risky as potential customers of a bank. A person familiar with different management concepts is apt to have applied some of them to her business.

Quality is a big concept today. It will remain a big concept as long as the business planet seems to shrink. People who don't know what quality is have a tendency to define it by saying it has something to do with the absolute best product or service. Actually, quality is defined as conformance to standards and is a terribly broad concept involving goal analysis and standards, production process analysis and standards, and human resource analysis and standards.

Organized structured systems and processes within an organization, whether it be very small or very large, are an indication of control. The managers are controlling the business versus the business controlling the managers.

Neatness

Neatness is a very obvious indicator. I have called on a lot of small retail businesses as a banker. Eventually, you end up in the back room next to the inventory. There is a small desk. That is where you can see the end result of neatness. If the store and the employees are neat and clean, then the tiny little office also is neat and clean. In all probability, that means its books are all neat and clean, too.

Personnel

Personnel selection indicates leadership ability on the part of the owners or senior management. Bright, positive, outgoing personnel had to have been hired by an individual who knew what he was doing. Employees who constantly chip in when not asked to or orchestrate internal employee events are the kinds of employees that drive a profitable company. Their presence is much more obvious in smaller companies.

CASE STUDIES

The following two case studies will help you understand how certain businesses do make money. The first case is about a camera store. It includes an income statement. The second case involves an advertising agency. This allows you to compare a retail business with a service business.

King's Kamera Store

The first time that Delores Weisner met Mike King was very awkward. In retrospect, she'll never forget it. The bank had just instituted an officer call program. She was going to have to start making sales calls on business customers. The thought of it made her very uneasy. Delores had been a branch manager for three years at Willoweed Bank, one of five banks in her tourist town of 15,000. Never had anyone talked to her about selling. That was certainly something she did not want to do. The image of her walking down the street with an attache case made her feel like some small-town, fast-talking, pots and pans salesperson. But the bank had made this selling process mandatory. They printed a list of local retailers she had to call on. Also, the bank provided a nice capabilities brochure describing the bank's services to businesses.

She picked King's Kamera as her first call. Having grown up in Wyman, she knew the owner, Mike King. She met him and his wife Dorothy at a local neighborhood meeting for city merchants. He is about 10 years older than she is. She thought it interesting how she grew up in a small town and thought she knew everyone. Then she met someone like Mike, who also grew up in the same town. Delores didn't know anything about him or his family, and they had very few mutual friends. It all made her wonder how small a small town really is.

Mike King started his business about five years ago. He always wanted to have a camera shop in the town in which he was raised. There was no other camera store in town and Wyman was part of the most heavily visited tourist area in the state. The time seemed right. Photography had always been Mike's hobby. He was a photographer for the Army during the Vietnam conflict, and when he got out, he worked in a processing lab for a commercial photographer and took night courses in commercial photography. After several years of lab work, he realized he wasn't going to be able to support a family on what he was making. Mike interviewed for a job in the photography department of a major corporation at a salary level just slightly lower than his existing salary, but with the promise of a promotion within 90 days. His gamble paid off. After two years, he was a staff photographer, earning a fairly good salary. But the work was boring: photographs of the executives shaking hands, photographs of machine parts as they came off the assembly line, photographs of the executives handing machine parts to each other, and on and on. Mike needed a challenge. It was provided to him by Ted Iris, a major camera corporation sales representative. He told Mike that his company's research indicated that Wyman could use a good camera store. When 175 Main Street opened up and Ted's company agreed to flexible payment terms for Mike, and Mike's parents loaned him part of the initial inventory money, King's Kamera was born.

Today, King's Kamera is a legal corporation doing close to $500,000 in sales. That's what Mike told Delores during her first sales call to King's. He was noticeably impressed that a bank was calling on him. "Nobody else has ever called on me, unless I owed money," he joked.

Delores learned that Mike banked with First Center State Bank, a large statewide bank created through several years of merging and purchasing of smaller banks. First Center State was the bank that a lot of businesses used. When Delores asked Mike if he was pleased with his bank, he indicated that he hadn't really thought about it. It was just another bank on Main Street. They hadn't really done anything for him except accept his night bags and send him statements.

"Is there something else a bank should be doing for me?" he asked.

"I would hope so," she replied. "Direct deposit. Sweep accounts for temporary cash excess. IRAs. Commercial loans."

"Whoa," he cautioned. "You and I don't even speak the same language. The only thing you said that I understand is loans. What are those other sweep things you're talking about?"

"Well, you've been in business now for five years, right?"

"That's right."

"Surely, from time to time you have found yourself with a balance in your checking account that you planned on using for growth in the near future, or to pay off a bill in 90 days, or some kind of situation where you didn't actually need that cash immediately. Is that right?"

"Well, I guess," he thought. "Yeah. So what?"

"Does your bank pay you interest on that excess balance in your account?"

"No. I just have a business checking account. Personally, we have one of those NOW accounts that do pay interest."

"So you might carry a few thousand dollars in your noninterest checking account for a few months?"

"Yeah. If I put it in my personal account, I'll get all screwed up."

"Mike, you could be earning up to 4 percent on that money. Otherwise you're paying the bank to keep large deposits for you. Do you happen to know what kind of average balances you keep?" Delores asked.

"Well, not exactly. Dorothy does the books. She'd know. Is that really important?"

"Just look at the numbers, Mike. If you're carrying $5,000 in your account that isn't doing anything for you, wouldn't you rather be earning, say, $200 on that money than nothing?"

"Well, of course. But you really should be talking to Dorothy."

"Maybe the three of us could talk at sometime convenient for you both."

True to his word (and not to Delores's credit) Mike called her at the bank a week later. [Dear reader, please understand that the odds that a customer will call you are remote, to say the least. But Delores lucked out!] Mike called her back and told her that he and Dorothy would be interested in talking with her. Delores suggested that they come into the bank, where they could have a certain amount of privacy. Delores also knew that the bank was her turf and all of her sales training taught her the advantages of selling in an environment that the seller controls, if possible.

By the time Mike and Dorothy came, Delores had talked to Ned Jefferson in Commercial Banking to find out what kind of questions she should be asking and the kinds of products that a mom-and-pop shop would, logically, need.

Without knowing anything else about the business, you should have some basic products in mind. Try prioritizing those products with the lead product first. What are they?

1. _____
2. _____
3. _____
4. _____
5. _____

The meeting was very helpful to Delores. Thanks to Ned, she knew the kinds of questions she should be asking. It seemed to Delores that the real key to the business working over the long run was Dorothy King. She guarded the books with zeal. She knew where every penny went and maximized her net-10 discounts as well as stretched her 30 days to the limit. Dorothy was very proud of figuring out how to increase their raw margin with major camera suppliers for 10 percent to 15 percent simply by paying within 10 days. "That's an increase in our margin of almost 30 percent," she stated proudly.

King's Kamera operates with Mike, Dorothy (part time), three clerks, and two part-timers. The store is a comfortable size, 2,100 square feet, for which they pay $24,150 per year. Both Mike and Dorothy wince at the rent, but it is in the middle of town with ample parking out the back door, a prime location. They are a bit concerned because the building they are in is rumored to be for sale. It contains 5,600 square feet. Delores probed to find out if Mike and Dorothy would be interested in buying it. Mike was. Dorothy considered it absolutely out of the question. "They probably want a half million for it. Where are we going to get that kind of money?"

The three full-timers made approximately $1,000 per month gross, each. The part-timers made about $100 per month, each. Taxes and payroll, Dorothy estimated, were 12 percent.

Delores's pencil began moving as she inconspicuously calculated. "15 percent margin. Doing $484,049. Gaad. That's about $72,000! How in the world do they pay their bills? Let's see, the salaries are around $36,000 plus another $10,000 for part-timers. Rent is $24,000. And they're not even paying themselves. How do they make any money?" Delores spent some time going over the figures. She finally called Mike and Dorothy and asked for another brief meeting.

At that meeting, she learned that the 15 percent margin that Dorothy squeaked out was for cameras only. And camera sales accounted for about 30 percent of the total. Mike indicated that the profit dollars came from lens caps, filters, gadget bags, picture frames, copies from their copy machine, passports, and the photo finishing that they farmed out.

"So they make 15 percent on roughly $145,000. I wonder what they make on the other $340,000? To pay Mike and Dorothy a salary, they're going to need to gross about half of that, about $170,000; $21,700 on cameras and $170,000 on other stuff would give them about $190,000. That would be about a 40 percent margin, overall," Delores mused.

Meanwhile, Mike had been secretly meeting with the owner of the building. They had talked about King's Kamera's purchasing the real estate. The owner told Mike that he knew the property was worth well over $500,000. Mike felt he might be able to buy it somewhere in the high $400s. But that meant having to come up with $60,000 to $80,000 up front and some very large monthly payments.

As part of Delores's monthly follow-through on her retailers, she happened to stop in to see Mike. Dorothy was chauffeuring for a soccer match and the store was slow. Mike told Delores about his desire to own the property.

"Do you own your house?" Delores asked.

"Well, we will in another 15 years."

"So you bought it 10 to 25 years ago?"

"That's right. I know what you're thinking, Delores. I might be able to use the collateral in the house. Right?"

"It's a possibility, Mike. I'll have to look into it. Actually, I'd like to look into everything on a more formal basis and consider King's Kamera as a full-service customer for our bank. That would mean you would have to provide us with some fairly substantial numbers."

"I don't know if they're substantial or not; but Dorothy keeps the most accurate books you'll ever look at. And we do pretty well. Let me put some information in the mail for you. I think we have an income statement that might be helpful."

Two days later Delores received the income statement in Figure 10–2.

F I G U R E   10–2

KING'S KAMERA Income and Expenses

Sales			$480,049.00
Gross profit			$187,219.00
Less operating expenses			
Payroll			
	Mike	20,000.00	
	Dorothy	16,000.00	
	Clerk 1	13,000.00	
	Clerk 2	8,150.00	
	Clerk 3	10,000.00	
	Pt. time	3,000.00	
	Pt. time	3,500.00	
Total payroll			$73,650.00
Rent			24,150.00
Advertising		2.5% of sales	12,101.00
Payroll taxes		15.00%	11,048.00
Store expense		2.03% of sales	9,826.00
Group insurance			1,800.00
Insurance		.92% of sales	4,453.00
Utilities		.73% of sales	3,534.00
Repair/Maint.		.42% of sales	2,033.00
Telephone		.32% of sales	1,549.00
Mtgs/Seminars		.35% of sales	1,694.00
Dues/Subscriptions		.20% of sales	968.00
Postage		.24% of sales	1,162.00
Legal acct.			2,500.00
Office expense		.06% of sales	290.00
Security		.13% of sales	629.00
Misc. taxes		.02% of sales	97.00
Total operating expense			151,484.00
Net profit/loss			$35,735.00

Additional Information on King's Kamera

Many camera stores fail for the following reasons:

1. Too hobby-oriented. Must be looked on as a business. Must be market-driven versus product-driven.

2. No respect for the margin. Not being aware of strict profit margins and having to pay the suppliers on time. There is a tendency for retailers to put cash in their pocket rather than in their cash register. The cash register pays bills. The pocket has a hole in it.

3. Weak product mix. Too many retailers ignore the small items, forgetting that those items, with their high margins, can create more profit dollars than the large-ticket items. A good point in this case study is the fact that King's makes more profit dollars on passport photos than on cameras because its markup on passport photos is about 10 times. The second most profitable item in the store is picture frames; a $10 frame can cost King's as little as $2.50.

4. Too price-sensitive. According to research on retail photo supplies, the most important criterion for purchasing a camera is professional, competent employees. The third most important criterion is price. Many small retailers believe the only way they can stay in business is to undercut the big discount retailers. That assumption will put a camera store out of business in three months.

5. No in-house photofinishing. Any camera shop without an in-house lab will find their backs against the wall too many times. It is said that photofinishing allows the camera store the luxury of selling cameras. Photofinishing will provide a 50–70 percent gross margin. It will cost about $125,000 to purchase the equipment; however, that money is easily borrowable through banks and through assistance programs provided by the manufacturer. A store needs 45 rolls a day to break even. Many stores the size of King's average 80 to 100 rolls a day.

Questions Regarding King's Kamera

All answers and further information can be found in Chapter 14, "Case Solutions," at the end of the book.

1. Is it an advantage for a business like King's to employ members of the family? Why? Why not?

2. What is the single largest expense in a retail business like King's? List it as a percentage of sales.

3. What is co-op advertising? Does it apply in this case?

4. What is the gross margin at King's Kamera?

5. How is King's Kamera doing? Is it making any money?

6. What kinds of things should the Kings be doing to improve their margin and strengthen their business?

7. If all salaries (except Mike's and Dorothy's) are $36,000, can they afford to pay themselves another $36,000?

8. Do you believe that $72,000 as 47 percent of its total operating expense is too high? Why?

9. Should they buy the building? Why? How?

10. What banking products and services would encompass a reasonable full-service banking relationship?

Lee Advertising

Dan Wilson is an aggressive branch manager for a $400 million thrift. He manages a $54 million branch. Senior management began a major push to get the branch managers involved in their communities to create sales within the local business communities.

Dan joined the local chamber of commerce. While he was at a chamber Business After-Hours function, he met Marilee Lewis. She is the owner of Lee Advertising. They spent almost an hour and a half together, informally chatting. Because she was an entrepreneur, Dan knew she would want to talk about her business. Dan was interested in talking with the owner of one of the fastest growing advertising agencies in the tri-state area and apparently Marilee was interested in talking to a banker. That's a combination that can be dangerous!

Lee Advertising started just 18 months ago with nothing. Marilee left Johnson Juices, a major packaged goods company, where she was a product manager and started her agency with one small project from Johnson. It must have been an amiable split for her to leave the company with some business. She indicated to Dan that both she and the company realized she could do more for the company on her own than being tied down with tons of bureaucratic paperwork. She still has a division of Johnson.

At present, Lee has $8 million in billings. She has 12 people on her payroll. Her approach to creating a strong ad agency was to spend money hiring the best people and not to cut corners. "In this business, you get what you pay for," she said to Dan. About six months ago, she hired a seasoned pro from the largest agency in town to run the account management side of the business. Dan was curious to know what someone like that was worth. Marilee hesitated briefly then said, "It's a six-figure package." Apparently, an agency should have a heavyweight account management person and a heavyweight creative person, both close to a hundred grand. Marilee was negotiating to bring the creative person on board. She just fired the old creative director, who wasn't able to carry his weight creatively because of the business's growth and the kinds of accounts she was pursuing.

A year ago she was pitching the local bank, which spent a couple of hundred grand a year on advertising. Now she is pitching a major regional bank holding company, which spends $3.5 million in advertising.

She has picked up two major computer hardware companies, a software company, a manufacturing company, two large management-development companies, and a couple of land developers. She is feeling the pressure to provide public relations along with advertising and marketing promotions. She knows a PR effort would entail hiring another big salary. It might mean starting a special PR company and offering a piece of the action to the person who would run it. Marilee would keep her hands out of it.

Dan asked her, "I don't know a lot about the advertising business. What does $8 million in billings mean?"

"That's what our clients pay for advertising. Actually, we never see that. A realistic figure for us is gross income. That's how much money comes in the door. It's usually about 20 percent of a client's billings."

"So that means you do about $1 million in sales."

"That's a fair estimate. Out of that we have to pay salaries, rent, telephone, insurance, all that stuff. Back in the old days," she continued, "agencies used to make 15 percent on all billings. That was it. I'd go broke today if I did that."

Presently, she is using a large bank to handle her banking needs. Luckily, she has some equity. She owns a house on a nearby resort that was left to her by her parents. She estimates it is worth about $500,000; there is no mortgage. She also owns a three-story brownstone in the heart of the downtown area. She bought it 15 years ago for a song.

Dan asked around when he got back to the office and found out she isn't married. She dates some fairly big-time guys, but not seriously. Mostly she works. She's in the office by 7:00 AM. and leaves at 9:00 PM.

Dan ran a D&B on her and didn't learn anything new about the business, only that her bank is the largest commercial bank in the area. Also he understands D&Bs and knows they're not entirely accurate. Small businesses can fudge their numbers easily.

Dan decides to ask Steve Principal, the commercial lending senior VP, if he can put Lee Advertising on his call list. Steve gets back to him and OKs it.

Now Dan has got to do a little math. Must estimate payroll. Figure out the kind of margin that $8 million in billings might return. Should learn a little about the advertising business so he won't look like a total fool when he talks to her.

From the regional office of the American Association of Advertising Agencies (AAAA), Dan was able to find out that agencies try for a 20 percent gross margin. That figure is called gross income, or sales, and 30 percent of sales should be operating expenses. The person in the AAAA office said, "The gross profit of an advertising agency should be 100 percent of the money available to operate the agency. That includes such items as salaries and rent." Dan figured that 20 percent of what they call billings would be gross income and the gross income is the money that would be used for salaries, rent, and overhead.

"Well, if that's the case," he mused, "she should have about $1.6 million for operating expenses and salaries and profit."

Two weeks later Dan received a phone call from Marilee.

"Dan, you're going to have to tell me whether a small bank like yours could do anything for me or not. I certainly would like to get my agency in a better position staffwise and that would mean money—in one form or another. Is this something we could discuss?"

"I'd like to pursue it, Marilee. I have done just a little bit of research, enough to know that I need to get some figures from you. Could you carve out some time for me to sit in your office and learn more about your business?"

Dan knew that he shouldn't try to get information over the phone. His phone is for appointments. Also, he wanted to see Marilee's agency.

A couple of days later, they met. Marilee explained that she didn't have current financials at that point. Her accountant was preparing them. Also she wasn't sure whether Dan's bank was the right one and didn't want to divulge any figures until she felt a little more comfortable.

"Our bank is very strong, Marilee. I brought along our latest annual report. I'm sure you have lots of these. We happen to be one of the most profitable savings banks in the state. We do have a commercial banking division and the person who heads it up, Steve Principal, used to be the senior lender for your present bank. Is our size an issue for you?"

"Not really. Especially now. I just want to make sure that I'm dealing with someone who knows about business."

"Well, I've been doing a little homework. As I get more and more information, I'll be interacting with Steve. We are not authorities on the advertising business, but we do know business."

Their conversation revealed the Lee Advertising had a gross income of $1.5 million. Marilee told Dan that 50 percent of her income is used to pay salaries, 20 percent is operating profit, and the rest would be overhead. That was what a financial consultant she had hired told her.

Her major concern was the cost of soliciting new business. Last year, she spent in the neighborhood of $300,000 soliciting new business.

"Whoa!" Dan said. "What in the world do you spend that kind of money on?"

"Dan, we were involved in pitching 14 different accounts. In today's advertising business, when you pitch an account, the client expects to see finished ads, none of this rough sketch stuff."

Dan mentally figured, "2 times 14 is 28. That's about $25,000 each."

Dan felt that was a little high, but then again what did he know? He certainly wasn't in that kind of business and Lee Advertising certainly was growing.

"Dan, I am too lean to grow. I need to develop a proactive approach to new business, but first, I don't have the time, and, second, I don't have the support to chase new business."

"Are you saying you need more people?"

"I certainly do. Not to open the doors. That's my job and I do it very well. I need some support to relieve me of my duties as an account executive on three accounts and the finance function in here."

"How many people are you talking about?"

"Three. I need a financial controller-type person. I need an account executive and I need a copy chief. That's going to cost me about $120,000. I look at that on a monthly basis. I see that as $10,000 per month."

"Marilee, do you have a business plan?"

"I certainly do. I also will be getting some complete financials, which I'd like to get over to you. My concern is that I'm in a rush. I need to move quickly. Is your bank the kind of bank that can spot an opportunity and run with it?"

"If everything looks positive, I'm sure we can move as fast as the next bank. How soon can you get me your numbers, a business plan, and a personal financial statement?"

"I'll have them delivered to your office by the end of the day tomorrow."

Additional Information on Lee Advertising
Reported gross income is $1.5 million.

Marilee is spending about $300,000 on new business, and that doesn't include salaries. Do we know what that $300K includes?

Of the total income, 50 percent should be used for labor and 20 percent should be operating profit. The rest is operating expenses (rent, telephone, client expenses, insurance, office equipment, supplies, etc.)

An advertising agency reports its billings as made up of media billings, retainers, and creative time. To standardize their reporting, agencies have elected to capitalize their retainers by multiplying them by 6.67 and reporting the new figure as billings. They do the same thing to creative time.

Here are some red flags:

1. The agency is showing a growing loss.
2. Their receivables are 90 days or over.
3. Their payables are 90 days or over.
4. The owner(s) have very little capital.
5. The owner(s) have few bankable assets.
6. Their client list is boring and full of dying industries.

Questions Regarding Lee Advertising
1. As Dan Wilson, what are the first five steps you are going to take with regard to preparing for the pursuit of Lee Advertising?
2. Simply explained, what is the gross margin in an advertising agency?
3. Just from the information provided to this point, how would you loan money to Marilee?
4. What is her monthly payroll?

5. What is the income from an $8 million agency?

6. What is the income from an $8 million bank?

7. Draw an organization chart for the top three levels of a small $5–8 million advertising agency.

8. What is Marilee's primary banking need in terms of product?

S U M M A R Y

1. Smaller community banks might have a commercial division with two or three loan officers. They should be called on to assist the branch manager rather than replace him.

2. The customer doesn't care about the features of a product or service. The customer is interested in what product or service is going to help make more money.

3. The small business owner is more bottom-line oriented than a large business manager because the small business owner has his personal holdings at stake.

4. Small business owners want to talk about their families as much as their businesses. And therein lies the secret to a banker's success in doing business with the small business person.

5. Businesses make money in two ways: by decreasing expenses and/or increasing sales; that is, bringing money in and spending as little as possible (so the owner can put more in her pocket).

6. Every sales dollar has three parts to it. One is how much you paid for the product you sold. That's called the cost of goods sold. The other is the total amount of money you spent actually running the business. That's called the operating expense. Now you add cost of goods sold and operating expense and if they are less than the dollars you received from your customers, then you made some money.

7. A margin is what you get when you divide the gross profit by the net sales.

8. Beyond the obvious dollars and cents of analyzing the ability of a small business to make money, three nonfinancial indicators you should look at are knowledgeable management, neatness, and personnel.

Managing Your Sales Efforts and Those of Your Internal Staff

Sales management is the process of motivating yourself to organize and accomplish an ongoing external sales effort. Also, it is your ability to motivate, organize, and accomplish a successful internal cross-selling sales effort. The most important part of any management effort is accountability. Performance must be accountable, otherwise it won't happen on a regular basis, and, as a manager, you will have little control over the success of the effort. You must measure productivity in individual, incremental segments to accomplish a successful sales effort.

Have you ever wondered why and how athletic prowess constantly improves? Won't there ever be a point in time when someone will never run faster than X? Sports are driven by success. The measurement of that success is the ultimate motivator. It's not just the total time it takes to run one mile; it's the time it takes to run the first quarter mile versus the last quarter so the athlete can pinpoint an area of improvement.

For many years, the business community would tell a salesperson that she sold $4 million; that used to suffice, just as the five-minute mile used to suffice. Then someone came along and said, "We are going to have to do better than our personal best. How do we do that?" We break the total into increments and analyze those increments. This is a quality approach to performance. It is the backbone of the quality movement worldwide. In essence, we are approaching sales from the concept of continuous performance improvement.

MEASURING SALES PERFORMANCE

As we have learned, there are various kinds of selling in retail banking. Some are measurable and some are not. There is much confusion still going on over what is sales and what is marketing. So, to set the record straight, let's go to Figure 11–1 where we illustrate the types of selling and outline the diagram:

I. Sales

   A. External selling

   B. Internal selling

      1. Convincing selling

      2. Cross selling

         a. Tuesday selling

         b. Thursday selling

F I G U R E   11–1

Types of Branch Selling

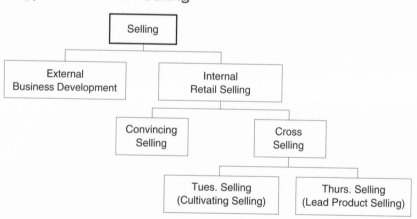

Measuring and Managing the External Sales Effort

External selling (A) has a model that allows us to incrementally break down the sales process from a task point of view. Let's develop that model from a management point of view. An external sales effort at most banks consists of most or all of the following steps:

1. Preapproach letter to a prospect.
2. Telephone call to letter mailing list.
3. Sales calls made based on telephone calls.
4. Sale made based on call.

We have determined that the average sales cycle for a branch manager calling on small retail businesses is approximately five months. The bigger the business, the longer the sales cycle.

Larger banks whose managers and regional managers are actively involved in external selling average one new business call each week. That means 52 new business calls each year. An aggressive effort that is organized will result in 37 percent becoming clients of the bank. That's about 19 new customers a year.

"But wait a minute!" you're saying. "I thought you told me there are banks whose branch managers are out 1.6 days per week selling. Surely one could make four calls during those 1.6 days? Four calls is 208 calls per year."

In actuality, branch managers call on existing clients as well as new business during their 1.6 days. Also, there are few banks whose managers do new business calls 1.6 days per week. It averages 52. That's a good safe number.

So 19 new business clients each year based on 52 personal sales calls based on 81 telephone calls. If your bank has an active direct marketing program, it will send out 100 letters for you to make 81 telephone calls. Or you can look at the 100 number as leads regardless of whether they were letters or personal referrals. From a management point of view, let's look at our numbers in Figure 11–2. This performance gauge tells us that the salesperson calls 81 percent of the leads. He gets a sales interview 63 percent of the time and 37 percent of the time lands the account. Are these figures good? Bad?

When I started compiling figures, I felt certain that I would soon have a database worth millions. Then I learned that different sized branches call on different sized businesses in different sized communities offering different kinds of financial services. The extremes run fairly far afield. So I began looking at mediums and means. Finally, I concluded that if, as a branch manager, you organize your time efficiently, you should set goals of 100, 81, 52, 19. That is what I use; then the bank modifies those figures.

F I G U R E   11–2

Performance Figures

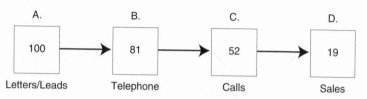

The important numbers are the percentages. It breaks down the improvement into increments. That way if one branch manager is at 19 percent (total leads to total sales) and another is at 11 percent, as a sales manager, I would want to examine the salesperson's ability to convert leads into interviews then interviews into sales. By breaking down the process, I can concentrate on the area in which the manager needs help.

Always evaluate performance over a period of time. The following sales incremental monthly log will help you to analyze and understand trends in your own performance.

Sales Incremental Monthly Log

Standards		81%	63%	37%
Week of	Preapproach (%)	Telephone (%)	Call (%)	Sale (%)

The top line gives you the standards that you work from. Your overall standard is 19 percent; that is, 19 percent of all leads become customers. So be careful about who your leads are . . . that they are qualified rather than random. You can build a weekly chart that will graph your ratios and reveal trends in your techniques. Analyzing those trends is the way you get better at selling.

Using Dollars to Measure Performance

Many banks prefer to use dollars. When I read figures that state business development activity as dollars, I wonder what kind of dollars—deposit dollars or loan dollars? Further, I wonder whether we are talking about sales or gross margins.

I have many concerns about managing sales performance using dollars unless the bank has the capability of determining an average gross-income figure for deposits and for loans. Only then are dollar figures viable performance indicators.

For those banks having the capabilities to measure dollars, the following formulas for sales performance might be of help:

1. *New Business Dollar Goals:* A total dollar amount to be achieved over 12 months.

2. *New Business Needed to Achieve Goal:* Total dollar value of all customers divided by total existing customers equals average customer value. Dividing average customer value into the goal for new business will give you the new business needed.

As a branch manager making business development calls, you will need to know how you are doing. Because you are a branch manager, your bank will assume that you are skilled in self-motivation or self-management techniques. Incrementally measuring your own performance is certainly a valid method of self-motivation.

Managing the Internal Sales Effort

The sales diagram at the beginning of this chapter revealed the following outline:

I. Sales
   A. External selling
   B. Internal selling
      1. Convincing selling
      2. Cross selling
         a. Tuesday selling
         b. Thursday selling

Internal selling (B) like external selling (A) can be incrementally measured. From a branch manager's point of view, measuring this activity is extremely important because you must learn how to spend more time actively selling to small businesses within your marketing area rather than overseeing your employees. Periodically analyzing sales performance reveals a lot about your platform personnel.

Are they just taking orders, that is, one product per customer, or are they selling? What products are they selling? Who is selling the most? Those kinds of questions enable you to manage your sales staff more efficiently. Let's explore an effective method of measuring sales activity.

Several years ago, I used to talk with bank executives about selling. Many would tell me that their people did not do it. Many would tell me, "They are selling like crazy!"

I would ask, "How do you know they are selling?"

"Because the branch managers tell me so," they would reply.

"How much are they selling?" I would ask.

"I don't know, but deposits are up."

I wondered quietly to myself, What in the world does that have to do with sales? But I never gathered the courage to actually ask. The fact of the matter was—back in the late 1970s—almost all banks' deposits were up, whether they were selling or not. So the assumption that just because deposits were up, sales were up was rather naive. If you owned the bank, wouldn't you want to know exactly how much money you were making from your selling effort versus your marketing effort? Obviously, we were once again talking incremental measurement processes.

So back in the seventies, we began experimenting with a unique concept that distinguished between sales and order taking. It also allowed the banker to further separate the marketing effort from the sales effort. I think that is very important. I wouldn't want the marketing department taking credit for my sales. Let them take credit for traffic; I will take credit for sales. That way when I want a raise, I won't have to ask for that raise based on the number of people that I was nice to. Instead I could base that raise on the exact amount of deposit money attributed strictly to my sales.

The first account a customer asks for is the result of marketing. The second and third products that the customer ends up with are the result of sales. Further simplifying this, we calculate sales each time a customer sits with us. I referred earlier to a sale as, "the second and third account, at a sitting." If we look at second accounts cumulatively, we are simply measuring accounts per customer, which is interesting marketing information but lousy sales performance information. Let's not trip over our enthusiasm!

Measuring Cross-Selling Efficiency

You must make sure that you can effectively evaluate your platform personnel's sales performance. Do this by analyzing the ratio of first accounts to second accounts. The following formula allows you to understand the relationship between first and second accounts and how to calculate this in your branch.

Step 1   Total first accounts
                 + Total second accounts (Cross sales)
                 = Total accounts

Step 2   Cross Sales Ratio $= \dfrac{\text{Total Accounts}}{\text{Total first accounts}}$

Ratios start at 1.00. That means no selling. For example, a CSR has 20 first accounts and no second accounts. If you calculate the ratio, you find it comes out to 1.00. A lot of platform people in banks with 1.00 think they are selling because they have a lot of traffic.

Depending on what products one counts as sales, an average ratio would vary. For the past 10 years, we have counted most products (including ATM cards) plus telephone transfers and direct deposits. If you use comparable products and your two CSRs have ratios around 1.50, they are doing a good job and you are being a good sales manager.

It is unfair to compare one branch to another because certain kinds of customers are easier to sell to than others. For example, if you are in a branch that has a ratio of 1.18 and you are counting all products and services, it would tell me one of two things: Either you are not doing a good job as a sales manager or the average age of your customers is more than 70.

The older your customer base, the lower your ratio is apt to be, even if you have the greatest salespeople in the world in your branch. Have you ever tried to cross sell off a passbook savings account or create five cross sales off a CD? Older customers still prefer the passbook savings. Even when you tell them they could earn more money by putting some of their savings in a CD, they still want the passbook with a growing balance they can see every month. If your branch is invaded by the blue-haired army, you are apt to have a low ratio, somewhere between 1.35 and 1.55.

If your branch caters to the yuppie market, your ratio could be as high as 1.90. Many CSRs in yuppie branches will go over 2.00! Numbers of accounts are higher in these kinds of branches even though the average dollar balance might be lower than the blue-haired branches.

Now someone is going to come along and chastise me for stereotyping individuals and making derogatory references to certain demographics. I do not do this with any malice—just a slight grin—since I have sold financial services to so many different kinds of customers. You are probably wondering how one could have a ratio greater than 2.00. Let me illustrate an easy scenario:

It is 9:00 AM. The doors of the branch just opened. It's Thursday. Busy.

A gentleman approaches my desk. He is in his early forties; wearing a business suit and little round glasses. Parts his teeth in the middle.

I stand and greet him. "Good morning. May I help you?"

"Yes, you may. We are moving here from Philadelphia so I am checking out banks near my new home."

"Welcome to the area. I'm Dwight Ritter," I say, holding out my hand. He shakes it. "Jack Barnes."

"Are you moving real close to here, Mr. Barnes?"

"Just up on Talbot Street."

"Well that will definitely make us closest to you. That should make it easier for you and your wife. Do you work locally or in the city?"

"Right in the middle of downtown," he says.

"I don't know if you already know this, but we do have three branches in the center of the city, as well."

"I didn't know that."

"So you must be interested in a checking account?"

"Right."

"Are you used to keeping a large minimum balance?"

"Well. I think we had to keep $700," he said searching the ceiling for information.

"Do you write a lot of checks?"

"Mortgage and other household bills."

"I see. We have a checking account where you only have to keep $500 as a minimum balance and you can write as many checks as you want. We'll also pay you 3.25 percent."

"Well, that's better than what I've got now."

"Exactly. Also since we are the closest bank to your work and your home, it might be advantageous to open an account while you are here."

"Might as well," he said reaching for his wallet.

After I got his account number and decided on checks, I presented him with signature cards for the checking account and one for the ATM card. He elected to open the account right away without a joint signature because his wife would not be moving to town for another six weeks. Just before he signed the ATM application, he asked what it was for. I explained that it was standard equipment on our checking account and it was free. He signed.

I asked him who he worked for in the city. It happened to be a business we had a direct-deposit relationship with. Because my bank uses customer direct-deposit forms in the branches, it was easy for me to have him sign up and save himself the agony of standing in line.

I suggested that with his ATM card, he could take money out of his checking account and put it into his savings account in the event he and his wife saved for vacations.

He thought that was a great idea and opened a savings account with $1,000 from his Philadelphia bank.

We chatted briefly about the town and the geographic area. I learned he had three children and rebuilds cars as a hobby. I sensed he was getting ready to leave and told him that from time to time my wife and I found ourselves with more month than money.

He looked at me blankly for about two seconds then chuckled.

"No matter how hard I try, either my wife or I will accidentally overdraw my checking account about once a year. It's that darned ATM card."

"Well you'd think, Dwight, that as a banker you wouldn't make those kinds of mistakes."

We both laughed. I told him about our overdraft protection. He signed up for it just before he left.

Now it is 9:15 AM. What do you suppose my ratio is? The first account was the checking account. Incidentally, I had to do a little convincing on that one. Didn't I? Then I cross sold an ATM card, direct deposit, a savings account, and overdraft protection. Four accounts. One order and four sales. One first account and four second accounts. I start the morning with a one-customer ratio of 5.00!

So, if my next two customers only open one account each, my ratio is still 2.33. One first account from my first customer and a first account from each of my next two customers. Therefore, I have three first accounts. Since the only customer I cross sold was my first customer, I total three first accounts and four second accounts and calculate my ratio as follows:

3 first accounts

4 second accounts

7 total accounts divided by 3 first account = 2.33

So, getting a high ratio might not be as difficult as you might think. As a matter of fact, an untrained, internal salesperson will make one cross sale out of every 10 customers through sheer luck.

You must remember that the ratio only applies to each time a customer comes in. It is not cumulative. When a customer comes in this month and opens a checking account and ATM and next month opens a savings account, that savings account becomes her first account for the new month. That is important to remember.

Yes, there are inadequacies on this kind of measurement system, but nothing is fair! I would hope that, at your age, you have begun to discover that. For example, a customer comes in and says, "I've got a lot to do today. I need a checking account and an ATM card. Also I'll need you to automatically take $100 each month out of that account and put it in a savings account. So I will also need a savings account. Can you do all of that for me?" You bet you can. That particular salesperson will probably write down that he opened a checking account and sold an ATM card, PDO, and a savings account. So, in that situation, the ratio is unfair. It is also unfair when a customer comes in and opens just one account. The salesperson struggles with no success to cross sell. The following month that same customer returns and opens one of the accounts the salesperson previously explained. Then the following month the customer returns again and opens yet another account the salesperson previously explained. In that situation, the ratio is also unfair. Life is unfair! Over a period of time, both life and our new sales management ratio seem to even themselves out.

Measuring and Analyzing Workload

Your salespeople will tell you they are so busy they don't know what to do. How do you know if they are? Now you will need some rules of thumb. For example, what is a busy CSR? How many first accounts does a busy CSR open? If you have two CSRs and their jobs are new account openings and sales—not operational duties—they should both be doing around 60 first accounts. Then, they are busy; not devastated, just comfortably busy. If you think about the 60 number, you realize there are 20 working days a month, so 60 is actually three each day. Well, we know that is not realistic, since some days are hectic and others are sparse. Also, to do 60 first accounts, a CSR will probably wait on about 180 people, helping customers with routine problems (which include their domestic problems, in many cases). We have found the traffic figure is slightly less than three times the first account figure.

So now one of your CSRs tells you she is so busy she can't see straight. You acknowledge that with a polite nod and check the number of first accounts she opens. You see the CSR opens 25 per month. This CSR needs some guidance unless, of course, she is doing a lot of operational work, pitching in on the teller line, and doing lots of loans. Otherwise a CSR who is doing 25 first accounts should not be telling you she is busy. She isn't.

What is interesting about the numbers so far is that you probably had no real facts to discuss with your staff with regard as to how busy they are. You have heard them complain that you are short-handed and that you need another CSR, but you had no way of really determining whether that was true. You could look at total branch deposits to determine if they are up over last year or not. But that isn't really helpful, because you don't really know how much work a CSR should be doing in the first place.

In a branch with two full-time CSRs, a couple of ATMs, and four full-time tellers, the CSRs should be doing between 50 and 60 first accounts. It means you have a branch around $30 to $35 million in assets. It also means that your branch is servicing around 300 customers per month at the platform. So it is a busy branch. If your CSRs are also cross selling, then the branch is probably profitable.

Deposit Money Related to Sales

We can examine more carefully this issue of profitability and its informal measurement from a sales management perspective by learning about deposit money for first accounts and deposit money for second accounts.

Two different kinds of monies come into the bank: either money taken from an existing account at your bank (transferred money) or money that comes from another bank (new money). Transferred money is money that your bank already has. Moving it into other accounts can positively affect the bottom line, but not as significantly as receiving new money from another bank. New money is more direct. It is easier to deal with and to understand its relationship to income or even profits.

If a customer comes into your branch and opens a checking account with $1,000 and the check that they hand you is from another bank, that $1,000 is termed first account new money. If the customer opened that checking account by taking $1,000 out of a savings account, that money would be termed first account transferred money. It is easy to see how new money could be more profitable than transferred money, since the physical transaction expense of moving money from one account to the other would be greater than just putting money into a new account.

Now let's assume that your customer has seen a need for investing some short-term cash. You uncover that need to sell her a six-month CD. She invests $5,000. The $5,000 check she gives you is also from another bank. That is called second account new money. If the check had come from your bank, it would be called second account transferred money.

In summary, the customer opens a checking account with $1,000 drawn from another bank and $5,000 also drawn from another bank. The sale was $5,000. The customer service order-taking amounted to $1,000. Assuming the customer leaves that money in the bank for awhile and the checking account has activity in it, the transaction would be profitable. Your customer service personnel can understand sales dollars from that point of view. It is very helpful for them to begin understanding their impact on the business.

From your point of view, as a sales manager, you want to focus on the amount of second account new money generated by your branch. You can track it over a period of time.

The graph in Figure 11–3 was developed by the manager of a $38 million branch; it shows the erratic nature of second account new money. The point of doing this for your staff is that if they are selling, you will begin to see an increase in this figure. Five percent of that figure could be construed to be the gross margin of the retail sales effort.

What is even more significant to the deposit dollars would be to tell CSR X that he accounted for $70,000 of second account new money. More realistically would be to let the CSR know that the amount of gross income he or she is bringing in is in excess of $3,500.

An interesting parallel to Figure 11–3 is how the sales ratios would equate. Let's look at Figure 11–4 where we overlay ratios for a compara-

F I G U R E   11–3

Second Account New Money

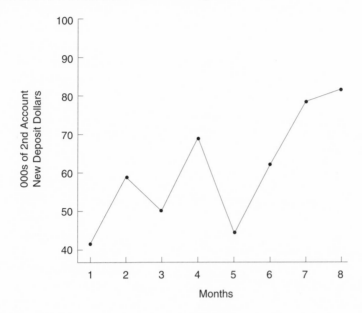

ble time period. Your ability to manage the sales efforts of your platform personnel is on the more active side of sales management.

COACHING YOUR INTERNAL SALES FORCE

Sales coaching is an art; your job is to help and guide your employees. We have a tendency to instruct and dictate. Coaching requires empathy and understanding. You will find it difficult, if not impossible, if you are not part of the cross-selling program in your branch.

In the beginning, some of your staff might tell you that the program is unfair—the tracking system is unfair, management doesn't understand, and they weren't hired to sell. You have heard them all before.

You will find that many salespeople object to being measured because they are afraid that they might not be able to sell. A natural reaction would be resistance to the one thing that could possibly prove that. So, in the beginning, much of your coaching will be soothing people's fears about accountability. Coaching should be done one on one. Don't do group coaching. It is not effective. If you do a group, you might as well

F I G U R E   11–4

Second Account New Money with Ratios

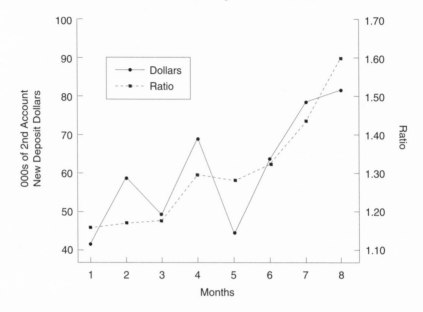

Months

have a sales meeting. Coaching needs structure. First, you observe a sale, making notes as you watch and listen. Second, when the CSR is not busy, you sit with her (or invite her into your work space). You ask, "How did you think that sale went?" As she answers, get her to think: How did the customer feel? Were there other sales opportunities? How would she have accomplished the sale in retrospect? How was her customer service? Third, tell the CSR what she did well either in customer service or sales. Fourth, tell her how her improvement will increase her sales performance. Fifth, always thank CSRs for the effort they are expending and underscore your willingness to support and assist.

People with low ratios need lots of structure. They need a written sales path and the words, so make sure they have them available. You might find, in the beginning, that you will have to spend some coaching time once or twice a week. As you begin to develop consistency, you can taper off on coaching to once a month.

Remember that effective coaching requires that you get specific. Talk about a specific sale. Have them recall exactly what they did. Any

"Oh, I don't know" is not acceptable. So I ask, "Who was the last customer you cross sold?"

"Gee, I don't know," the CSR starts to say, hoping I might drop the subject.

"Seriously," I push. "I want to know."

"Well, let's see. Uhmm, this morning I had a student come in and want a student checking account."

"Was it a male or female?"

"Male. Why?"

"Just curious," I shrug. "So what did he say?"

"Said he wanted a student checking account."

"What did you say?"

"I asked him if he had ever had one before."

"And?"

"He said he hadn't. I knew that by just looking at him."

"So what did you say?"

"I told him that chances are he would overdraw a checking account a lot."

"Why's that?"

"Well they do. Students open checking accounts and overdraw them. I always get them to open a savings account. That's where mom and dad should send their checks. Then the students should take only what they need, on a monthly basis, and put it into the checking account. This forces them to use bank accounts properly and really cuts down on overdrafts."

"That's a great idea." I exult.

"Yeah. It works well. Also, I will usually sell them a student Visa because it has automatic overdraft protection on it and will cover most overdrafts. The moms and dads love you for it. The bank doesn't have such big overdrafts each week."

"So at the end of that sales situation, what did you have?" I ask.

"Uhh. My first account was a savings account. I had two sales on top of it. A student checking and a student VISA."

"Hey. That sounds pretty good. What about ATMs?"

"Depending on the student. I'm still a little leary of kids with ATMs unless their parents want them to have it. So I don't push them."

Get specific. If you can't coach right after observing a sales session, start talking about their last sale. Find out what they said. Then what the customer said. Encourage them. Be supportive. Be impressed. Make suggestions. Also ask your staff to provide coaching to you on a monthly basis. They should see your results and internalize the kinds of help you might need to more effectively cross sell.

Conducting Successful Internal Sales Meetings

Depending on the kind of support you receive from your bank in sponsoring bankwide or regional sales meetings, you will need to reinforce their efforts with weekly sales meetings. If you work for a bank that has decentralized the sales effort totally into the branches, you should hold weekly sales meetings and quarterly sales extravaganzas. Weekly sales meetings should be short, 10 minutes, not more—usually less. The longer the meeting, the more your staff will dread showing up. If the meeting is brief, and at the beginning of each meeting you remind your staff that you want this to last just a half hour or so, they will look forward to the sessions. Have them before the branch opens. Many managers prefer Saturday morning. Review last week's sales. The following outline can be helpful:

    I. The weekly goals (ratios only).

    II. Individual performance (ratios only).

       A. Impact of new (or revised) products.

       B. Problems or concerns of the staff.

       C. Problems or concerns of the manager.

    III. Analyze cumulative second account new money.

       A. Forecast what is needed to meet monthly goals.

    IV. Special awards, commendations, and so on.

From time to time, it is good to bring in an outside speaker, either the bank's overall sales manager or a hot shot salesperson from another branch, or even an outside salesperson from a retail establishment to discuss how they cross sell. Periodically breaking the monotony of a weekly sales meeting keeps your staff motivated.

Motivating Your Staff

The idea of motivating your staff has been around forever; around so long and used so little that we don't know what it means. Motivation became a word without a meaning. When you use a certain word for so long and give it so many different meanings, it loses its identity. The word *motivation* has lost its identity. People feel it is almost mystical. They assign various values to it. Businesses hire enthusiastic speakers to come in and motivate the troops. I think what many businesses want are inspirational stories—maybe some secrets so their staff will be more enthusiastic—but motivation doesn't work that way. Many managers look for short-range fixes.

If I were to give a terrific motivational speech, it would only serve to provide one small piece of a very complex puzzle known as motivation. The Japanese approach to this concept of motivation is an ongoing, frequently highlighted, long-term process. Because of their approach, they do not have the employee turnover, lagging productivity, and sky-rocketing training costs found in the United States.

A typical Japanese approach would be to outline a series of reoc-curring events, all designed to meet specific targets. Those targets could be sales, production, turnover, or specific skill enhancement.

So motivation, then, is like breathing; that is, it's an action-reaction process. I breath in to breath out. Or vice versa. One thing depends on another thing happening. If nothing happens, then nothing will result. If you don't breath in, you can't breath out.

The U.S. system of motivation is like buying one inhale, thinking that the rest will happen automatically. Smart managers realize that you must make the individual's inhales happen. So motivation is not an end result, but a process that can never end. From your point of view as a manager, you should constantly be motivating your staff using proven motivators. What are they? Food, money, sex, success, inspiration, and variety. If it is possible to relate those six motivators to a common theme, the commitment to belonging will be greater.

The commitment to belonging is, at last, a definition of the word *motivation.* Psychologically, all human beings gravitate toward pleasur-able happenings. Your mind will naturally guide your behavior toward a preconceived pleasurable path. One that is risk-free. That's what your mind is trained to do: To find happiness without enduring any pain. What an assignment!

You have different biochemicals in your thinking system that are released through your pituitary gland at the base of your brain. These bio-chemicals produce energy. Failure or fear of failure produces lethargy, depression. Your job as a manager is to reinforce the positive energy built into our systems. That means dealing with failure or employees' preconceived notion of failure. You can do that by de-emphasizing the consequences of failure. I use this line, "It is easier to apologize then to ask for permission."

I want my employees to try things, to come up with ideas, regardless of whether they are good or bad. I want my employees to know that I need help, otherwise they will have to do things my way (what a dreadful thought!). To get a "commitment to belonging," my employees need to see me. I must be visible and available. I should make time to lunch with them. I should expose them to my style and personality. Management must be available. Many refer to this as "walk your talk." Spend time around the teller area. Talk to your platform personnel. Ask for their help, their input.

CASE STUDY OF POSEY COUNTY BANK AND TRUST'S BRANCH MANAGER

Donna Griffen is branch manager of Posey County Bank's Evansville office. Things have changed a lot around the bank in the last three years since Donna was promoted to branch manager. Senior management decided the bank should start thinking like a retail business. The words *sales culture* have been thrown around. Donna's not real sure what it means. In weak moments, she decides it must mean she has to go to another sales training class. Surely there must be more to it than that, she ponders.

Posey County Bank is a member of GreatBankNet, a multibank holding company with assets of $8 billion. Each of the banks maintains a certain amount of autonomy—name, management, and so forth. Donna's branch is the oldest branch in the Posey County system. It used to be the main office. With its centralized location in downtown Evansville, this is clearly a branch that the bank cannot afford to lose. This branch, politically, is one of the top branches in the system for a branch manager. Donna has her eye on the branch administrator's job or something close to it.

The branch has been hectic lately. John Paine quit a month ago. That really killed her. He had the best ratio of her three CSRs. He was even able to take some of the load off of Donna with regard to doing some external calls. John loved making external calls. He quit because he found another job that paid a lot more money than the bank, almost 50 percent more. John had been with the bank for just over 18 months. What a loss. His input in terms of second account new money represented 80 percent of the total monthly figure. Donna's going to have to work real hard to replace him.

Her other two CSRs are Madeline Scott and Minnie Jo Burris. Madeline has been with the bank for 28 years. She used to be executive secretary to old man Madison, the last of the original Madison family to preside over the bank. Getting Madeline to cross sell is practically impossible. Just last week, she told Donna that she thought this whole selling thing was "a crying shame, and an unfair, opportunistic thing to do to their loyal customers." Her cross-sales ratio is less than luck. But every Thursday, there are about five people waiting to see her, all day long. Madeline knows that if she weren't there, the bank would lose some very valuable customers. She has told Donna that a number of times. When Donna tries to push Madeline, she calls Arch Turner, the president, and complains. Then Donna hears from the person in charge of retail banking that she should not be so hard on Madeline. At about this point, Donna throws her hands into the air and stifles a loud scream. Madeline knows. She sort of smirks at Donna for a few weeks. Donna fumes.

The other CSR, Minnie Jo Burris, is 21 years old. She started as a teller about six months ago. Donna hired her because a friend of the marketing director at the bank used to work with her at an insurance agency in town. Minnie Jo is adjusting to the sales culture in what Donna thinks is an average way. Her ratio is average. Her effort is average. Her knowledge of the product is average.

Donna also sells. When she has the time, she can keep up with John in terms of ratios and deposit dollars; she had a 1.73 last month. But hiring, managing, training, and all of the operational things associated with the branch have kept her too busy to spend much time selling. Not only that, but the bank also expects her to meet weekly with her personnel and discuss sales productivity. She did it once. Everyone in the branch decided it was a waste of time. Donna always says she has her branch sales meetings. Why start trouble, she muses.

Donna also manages five tellers; two are part time and three are full time. The three part time are new. Since Minnie Jo was promoted to CSR, Donna had to find a new teller. It wasn't new to Donna since she has been turning over tellers at a rate of three out of five per year. Donna's average is right where the bank as a whole is.

A couple of months ago, the bank started an officer call program. Just what Donna needed. The person in charge of commercial lending has assigned each branch manager certain companies on which to call. Donna has to call three noncustomers each week and begin a sales cultivation process. In addition, she has to call on five existing customers each month. Servicing they call it. It was easy with John helping her.

If the branch managers do not turn in forms explaining the status of their calls, they receive a polite call from Arch Turner asking them why they didn't make their calls and encouraging them to not miss another call that week. The pressure is on!

The bank has a complicated system of incentives. CSRs are paid on the basis of their ratio: $2.00 per hundredth of a ratio point. Tellers receive referral points toward prizes or cash. Customer service is monitored via mystery shoppers and rewarded with cash, vacation days, or both. Branch managers receive monthly bonuses based on total factored income for the bank. Donna has been averaging about $415 per month. There are a couple of branch managers making twice that figure each month. But they are assisted by a couple of members of their staff. Donna is not eligible for the cross-sales compensation. Minnie Jo receives, on the average, about $50 per month in sales compensation. The average teller is receiving $25 per month in referral compensation and someone in the branch will hit the mystery shopper every third month to the tune of $25.

Donna's husband, Ted, was just laid off at the local petrochemical company. He was a shift foreman with 20 years of seniority. It appears that the local union reached an impasse with the management of the company; after lots of bluffing, a major strike took place, followed by new negotiations and severe cutbacks. Ted, unfortunately, was in the wrong place at the wrong time. The union has assured him that he will get the next available job in the plant. "It's just a matter of month," they claim. Meanwhile Ted is at home and very stressed; he is taking it out on the children.

Rumor has it that the bank is going to streamline the entire retail delivery process by giving all CSRs new computers and changing the teller terminals to a more advanced configuration capable of speeding up transactions. This rather than hiring another teller!

Donna is part of a conversion project team and has been asked to attend a one-week course in New York City. Ted has said that she may not go. The director of retail banking has said that she must go. Furthermore, she is expected to maintain her present sales ratio over the next quarter; historically, the next quarter is the worst of the year. Ted thinks that

Donna is taking advantage of him because he is out of work. She is expecting him to fix breakfasts and dinners and to clean.

Think about this case study briefly. Internalize in your mind the stress that Donna is under. Is it more than yours or less? Is this case study realistic from your point of view? How would it differ?

In Chapter 14 there are work sheets and answers to these questions and the following ones. If you have read the book carefully, you know that all of the answers to the questions are contained in one of the chapters.

Questions Regarding Posey County Bank and Trust

1. What is the size of Donna's branch in deposits?
2. What is John Paine's ratio?
3. If John is responsible for 80 percent of the branch's second account cross-sold money, what do you suppose Minnie Jo is selling?
4. What is Minnie Jo's ratio?
5. What is Madeline's ratio?
6. What is the total of nonsalary sales compensation in the branch?
7. How is Donna going to motivate Minnie Jo?
8. Should Donna be selling more? If so, what can she sacrifice?
9. If you are Arch Turner, what would you need to know about your branches?

S U M M A R Y

1. The most important part of any management effort is account- ability. Performance must be accountable, otherwise it won't happen on a regular basis and, as a manager, you will have little control over the success of the effort.
2. Measuring sales efficiency based on a branch manager's exter- nal sales effort involves the knowledge and understanding of their incremental progress. The following research provides a base line: when 100 preapproach letters are sent, 81 telephone calls result, 52 visits, and 19 sales. (See Figure 11–2.) This per-

formance gauge tells us that the salesperson calls 81 percent of the leads. He gets a sales interview 63 percent of the time and 37 percent of the time lands the account.

3. For those banks that have the capabilities to measure dollars, the following formulas for sales performance might be of help:

   a. *New Business Dollar Goals:* A total dollar amount to be achieved over 12 months.

   b. *New Business Needed to Achieve Goal:* Total dollar value of all customers divided by total existing customers equals average customer value. Dividing that figure (average customer value) into the goal for new business will give you the new business needed.

4. The following formula will help you understand the relationship between first and second accounts and how to calculate this in your branch.

Step 1   Total first accounts
                  + Total second accounts (Cross sales)
                  = Total accounts

Step 2   Cross Sales Ratio $=$ $\dfrac{\text{Total Accounts}}{\text{Total first accounts}}$

5. An active, sales-oriented customer service representative will wait on 180 customers, open 60 first accounts, and sell 30 products or services (3:2:1).

6. Two kinds of deposit monies come into the bank: either money taken from an existing account at your bank (transferred money) or money that comes from another bank (new money).

7. Sales coaching is an art. Your job is to help and guide your employees. We have a tendency to instruct and dictate. Coaching requires empathy and understanding.

8. Branch managers should conduct short weekly sales meetings of 10 minutes, not more.

9. The six motivators are food, money, sex, success, inspiration, and variety. These result in creating a commitment to belonging.

CHAPTER 12

Using Incentive Compensation for Salespeople

By the mid-eighties, bankers began talking about incentive compensation. They weren't real sure what it meant back then, but that has never deterred bankers in the past. Many banks were selling multiple consumer banking products by the mid-eighties. Bank employees were beginning to say, "I wasn't hired to sell. Now I am selling. How come I'm being paid basically the same?" That dialogue opened up the primary issue as to whether a bank would be willing to pay additional income to certain employees based on sales performance or not.

Before we discuss the performance aspects of sales commissions, let's discuss the organizational logistics of commissions. In actuality, creating sales commissions is easy. The difficult part is senior management deciding under whose umbrella this issue resides. Is it a function of the retail banking group or is it a salary administration function under human resources?

Historically, many incentive schemes such as giving CSRs a couple of dollars for getting consumers to sign up for ATMs or something of that nature, falls under the realm of the retail banking group. Those kind of promotions come from marketing and are executed by the retail group. Rarely does human resources get involved at that level. But when we start talking about an ongoing system of sales commissions, suddenly we are into salary administration.

If salary administration understood the concept of sales cultures and the general atmosphere of the branches, it would be easier for the branches to internalize the need and assist in the execution. This is not to imply that they don't. Some do and some don't. Once again, this struggle between these two areas slows down or even kills a program designed to control and manage performance through incentive compensation.

Let's get back to the issue of this chapter: commissions. Some banks are for this idea and others are not. Those that do not favor this compensation issue express concern that it will create undue competition among employees and the only one who will suffer would be the customer. They are concerned that overly eager bank salespeople would sell products to customers that they do not really need just to get commissions. Another good point. However, if your bank implements a sales culture in the right way, your staff will be extremely sensitive to the twin issues of taking advantage of the customers and co-workers. It is entirely up to the sales culture in the bank. *If you think that a sales culture is sales training, then do not implement any kind of incentive compensation.* If you don't know what sales culture means, you shouldn't even consider incentive compensation. If you do understand sales cultures read on.

Many banks will experiment with sales compensation by running special promotions and paying employees X dollars on the number of over 50 checking accounts they sign up. After the promotion, they drop the incentive program. Some bankers will think it was worthwhile. Others decide they would have gotten the same result without having paid commissions.

I believe banks need to either commit to a sales-incentive program or never talk about it or experiment with it. If a bank is convinced that incentive compensation is the way to go, it should announce that from now on it will pay its sales personnel on the basis of a salary and commission. The bank does not have to state exactly how that commission will be calculated, only that it has decided to pay commissions.

You have to make that clear; if you don't, your sales staff becomes confused. They don't believe there really is an incentive system. Management has a tendency to pay piddling amounts spasmodically and, eventually, it negatively impacts (once again) the issue of the sales culture. Carefully define the parameters of the commission so that those parameters are flexible and you can vary the commission based on the kind of income your bank needs each month. And, remember to

1. Tell the employees that there will be a sales-incentive compensation program.

2. Define who will be eligible for it.

3. Describe the general nature of the compensation method.

4. Report to the staff every month.

5. Pay rewards every month.

COMMISSION SYSTEMS

There are a number of commission systems; however, I'm going to discuss three: *ratio commissions, promotional incentives,* and *dollar-value commissions.* Within those three systems are variations. But remember those names.

Let's go back a bit and recall the different kinds of branch selling, as shown in Figure 12–1. They include external selling, convincing selling, and cross selling.

Of those three approaches to selling in branch banking, we could fairly and reasonably determine a method of payment for sales performance for external selling. For example, pay the external call officer on the basis of the number of calls closed to the number of calls made (ratio commission). In the previous chapter, I outlined methods of measurement for external selling: by numbers of calls (ratio commission) and by dollars (dollar-value commission). Depending on the generosity of the bank, a sales-compensation package can be tied to any of those measurement vehicles.

F I G U R E   12–1

Types of Branch Selling

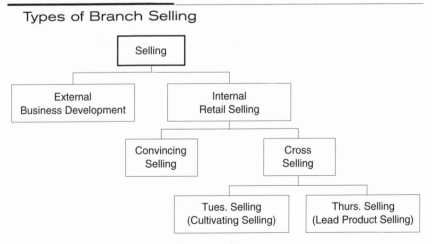

I have found it more effective to incent an external salesperson on the basis of numbers of sales presentations. In truth, many bankers have difficulty conceptualizing their individual impact on the bottom line, or even more simply, understanding how much of a $5,000 average balance on a commercial DDA is income. So I have steered my efforts at raw performance: How many sales calls did you make? How many of those calls did you convert to customers? The relationship of those two questions I would represent as a ratio and pay the external salespeople on the basis of that ratio. That is a ratio commission.

Once I have built a commission system based on a ratio, then I can begin promoting individual products or approved loans by paying the ratio commission plus the promotional incentive. Using this manner, the sales-commission concept stays in place and you have the freedom to introduce promotional incentives and drop them without disturbing the culture. Next, let me present a couple of incentive plans based on that previous concept of ratios of effectiveness and then add-ons.

Situation 1

Salesperson A made 10 calls each month for four months. All of the calls were on prospective customers, not present customers. The salesperson closed four calls by the end of the quarter. Here's how I would look at them:

$$\frac{\text{Calls, 40}}{\text{Sales, 4}}$$

Salesperson A is selling at a 10 percent rate. The bank pays that salesperson $4.00 for each percentage point of success, or $40.00 (which is not very good). That commission is based entirely on the ratio of sales to calls. It would be a ratio commission.

Situation 2

A customer service representative has a monthly cross-sales ratio of 1.66 (see page 159 for the calculation of this ratio). The bank has agreed to pay $2.00 for each hundredth of a cross-sales point each month. Therefore, this customer service representative will receive $132.00. Again this commission would be based entirely on the ratio of first accounts asked for to cross sales. It would be a ratio commission.

Situation 3

A loan officer made $300,000 of approved loans for a month. The bank instituted a dollar-value commission system that pays .5 percent (.005) for every approved loan. That loan officer made $1,500.

Situation 4

My bank is introducing a new product. We have decided to pay every plat-form person a $2.00 promotional incentive for each new product they open.

Those are the three incentive systems, in a broad, simplified way. Now let's mix them up. As I explained, my concept of an incentive pro-gram that works within the psychological framework of a sales culture is a ratio commission that always is in place, supplemented from time to time by other incentive schemes.

Let's go back to Situation 1. Once I have implemented my ratio com-mission, I will pay a 2 percent dollar-value commission bonus on the approved loan value to business customers. So that salesperson might have gotten $150,000 of approved loans, earning her an additional $3,000.

The point here is that I never eliminate the concept of ratio com-mission—that stays. I can eliminate my dollar-value commission bonus-es any time I want, depending on the need for loans versus deposits.

I can vary my ratio commission depending on whether I want it to (1) merely supplement a traditional salary, (2) enhance a frozen salary, or (3) totally replace a traditional salary.

Your bank should develop a sales-incentive strategy that would outline those three pay alternatives. In the first alternative, you simply implement an incentive compensation program for the sales staff that does not affect its existing pay schedule or impact its performance appraisals. Most familiar here is a competitive salary plus a percentage based on the cross-sales ratio as illustrated by page 159 called Situation 2. This alternative can be implemented fairly easily without disrupting salary administration.

The second alternative is to freeze the salaries of all who participate in the sales-incentive program. That salary would no longer be impacted by merit raises. It would simply remain a constant. (It can be periodical-ly affected by standard-of-living increases, depending on the approach by the bank.) All incentive programs, whether ratio- or dollar-based would be add-ons.

The final alternative is to create either a salary draw plus commission or a straight commission. The draw concept requires determining the average monthly salary of a salesperson. Let's say it was $1,500 per month. We institute our draw at two-thirds of the monthly salary, or $1,000 per month. If the salesperson earns more than the draw, the bank can decide to let the draw run for three months or accrue a debt (which is terribly cumbersome and an administrative nightmare!). With straight commission, the salesperson earns a commission (however it is orchestrated) on what she sells. There is no salary and no draw. This method can produce salespeople earning more money than your CEO or salespeople who earn nothing.

Mortgage salespersons have been known to be straight commission people. Some commercial lenders have been known to be on draw plus commission. Most retail banking has been conservative and stayed with competitive salaries supplemented by ongoing methods of performance incentive.

People ask me which method I think is the best. Being the consummate politician that I am, I say, "I don't know. It depends. Some work well. Some don't. Some work well where others don't. It just depends."

SUMMARY

1. Incentive compensation oftentimes creates a problem between the retail banking group and human resources. The question of who decides this issue of compensation can slow down the process.

2. If you don't thoroughly understand what a sales culture is, you shouldn't even consider incentive compensation.

3. Once you decide to implement a sales-commission system, you should:

   a. Tell the employees that there will be a sales-incentive compensation program.

   b. Define who will be eligible for it.

   c. Describe the general nature of the compensation method.

   d. Report to the staff every month.

   e. Pay rewards every month.

4. There are three kinds of commission systems: (1) a ratio commission, (2) a promotional incentive, and (3) a dollar-value commission.

5. The three types of sales compensation are (1) traditional salary, (2) commission draw, or (3) straight commission.

Improving Managing Skills

For the past 20 years, I have been in and out of bank branches and boardrooms.

I had dinner not too long ago in Denver with a banker who had just joined his third bank. We were talking about this process of implementing a sales culture and the overall complexity of it. He told me, "Dwight, this is my third total sales culture. That's true! I've been involved in these kinds of things now for eight years." He said that in a very prideful way, almost as if no one had touched those kinds of numbers.

Since I went into business 27 years ago, I have been involved in more than 600 sales cultures and thousands of sales training programs. I have made large errors that I prefer not to admit! I have had successes that I prefer to admit!

The single area that is most difficult to define, talk about, and teach is that of managing. Over the past few years, some rather brilliant people have begun to make some very valid and interesting inroads into the field of management.

MANAGEMENT VERSUS LEADERSHIP

One issue in particular is management versus leadership: *You can't manage someone into battle; they must be led.* Explaining the difference with that simple statement makes one realize that leadership and management are two different skills. In banking, it can be said that our branches are overmanaged and underled. We have many well-trained tacticians and few impulsive risk takers.

Sound military hierarchy is based on management. But getting people to die for you is based on leadership. Some processes are managed; some are led. The differences are vague, at first, but once you get into the thinking patterns, they become clear. Leadership creates change; management creates priorities. Change versus priorities.

With the emergence of large complex organizational structures filled with process systems, the need for well-organized human producers became paramount. These producers were master planners and schedulers. They could conceptualize a manufacturing process and determine the various stages of the operation. They could organize what had to happen first and make a listing of the elements. Through trial and error, this skill became more refined and accurate. We did notice that it began to break down with the issue of human behavior. We couldn't quite treat that in such a black-and-white way as the process. We knew that people were important and that the process couldn't really happen without the people.

A number of new fields began to emerge in the mid-eighties. The clarification of employee involvement. The understanding of quality. The psychology of team-building relationships and gain sharing. Humankind began to realize that it had to define the psychology of productivity as well as the process itself. Since the process had changed fairly naturally over the years and was controlled via this field called management, humankind assumed that the execution of behavioral change could also be controlled by the same field. And so we struggled and sputtered.

Even though leadership is a discipline and management is a discipline, they are not necessarily related. Entrepreneurs have a tendency to be good leaders. They hire good managers. Companies that survive and thrive through crises are generally run by good leaders. Companies that steadily grow and stay in the same business are run by good managers.

A good example was Swift & Company, a Midwest meatpacker. Managed by the same family for years, it began to experience difficulty as the market changed and its competition changed. They promoted Don Kelly to president from corporate controller. His job was to change the company to fit into the new competitive environment. Kelly was a leader and slowly reshaped the company until it wasn't really in the meatpacking business at all, but in the business of buying and selling companies. Swift had become Esmark, Inc., buying and selling companies in the food, chemical, energy, and textile industries. Don Kelly was clearly involved more in change than in priorities. Yet Don Kelly saw himself as a financial manager.

Let's examine some management processes and compare them to leadership processes:

Manager	Leaders
Plan and budget	Set directions
Organize and staff	Align personnel
Control and solve problems	Motivate and inspire

The tasks of goal setting, strategies, organization charts, and job specs are the natural tendencies of managers. The tasks of ideas, vision statements, objectives, changing strategies, risk taking, and exploring are the natural tendencies of leaders.

The major difference is in one group's ability to motivate. That means providing the framework for motivation such as employee gatherings, contests, suggestion boxes, and team performances, as well as actually being in there with the troops, affecting people's feelings about themselves and their jobs. Involving the staff is a major motivational concept.

Leaders are on the shop floor. A good branch leader will be totally and visually multiskilled. He will fill in as a teller or customer service representative and also force the staff to become multiskilled. Leaders make themselves very visible.

Leaders are not good delegators, but everyone has been telling them that for so long that they have a tendency to overdelegate at times, that is, to give people tasks they cannot handle. Good leaders think that everyone can become a good leader. Good managers are skeptical that anyone can become a good manager.

I often get criticized for suggesting that good leaders are like killers. Society doesn't really understand what makes them kill or why they kill. They get a lot of press, but the true psychology of how they think is still unclear. The difference is that we are trying to get rid of killers, not leaders.

Successful companies must learn how to define who its next leaders are. They can do that by creating challenging opportunities for younger employees and watching them to see how they exist within those opportunities.

To simplify this process, I have devised the grid in Figure 13–1. It seems that everytime I put titles or adjectives in those 16 boxes, I change them. Anyway, for now, make two copies of the leadership/management

F I G U R E   13–1

Leadership/Management Matrix

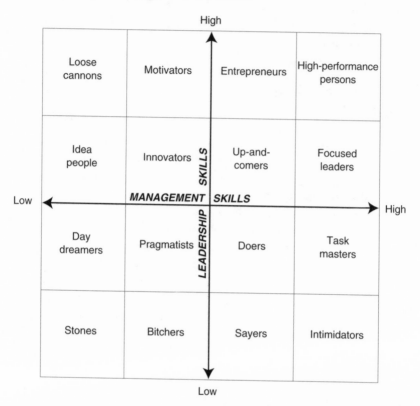

matrix. You will need one for yourself and one for your employees. Now think of yourself and what you do. Shade every box that best describes you (and you must be honest). Don't shade what you would like to be, shade what you are.

Now make a list of all the descriptive adjectives that are shaded. Pass that list to your employees along with a copy of the grid. Have them put a check next to every adjective they think best describes you. The three adjectives with the most check marks would indicate your propensity toward a balance between management and leadership.

If you are in the upper half of the major square, you tend toward leadership. The lower half, you tend toward management. As you can tell, the upper right-hand small box is the ideal that you should strive for. This unique mixture would provide just the right amount of management and leadership to the employees. So if, for example, your three leadership management characteristics are intimidator/task master/doer, then it indicates that you need to work on leadership traits. You should concentrate more on one-on-one communications, motivation, talking to your staff about vision statements, and trying to figure out innovative ways to increase sales in your branch.

If, on the other hand, you are a loose cannon/idea-oriented/innovator, you need to concentrate more on schedules, sales results, staffing, sales goals, and the operational aspects of your branch. It's a balance. That is the key. If you find yourself in the upper right-hand quadrant, then, logically, you must learn to understand and describe those skills that would be needed to offset your lack of management. As an effective branch manager in any consumer society, you must learn and develop more leadership knowledge, hence, characteristics.

TRAITS OF GOOD BRANCH MANAGERS

Some months ago, we began a large research project by talking to branch employees. We were trying to determine which traits branch employees thought good branch managers possessed. It was most informative.

We found six distinct traits exhibited by effective branch managers:

1. Experienced
2. Multiskilled
3. Good prodders
4. High energy levels
5. High standards
6. Innovative

Let's briefly examine these traits. Perhaps the most interesting comments related to the fact that good branch managers had experience in the branches, that they worked their way up. That means they started out as tellers and worked their way up to branch managers. It also meant that the branch manager could easily fill in as teller or customer service rep.

As I visit many branches, I see managers with beautiful platform automation systems on their desks. When I ask them about it, probably half of those managers don't know how to use it, or they don't use it to open accounts. In many branches where the manager had the system in her office, one of the CSRs didn't have one. Now where is the logic of that?

Trait number 3 is good prodders. I stretch that word to encompass the positive aspects of prodding. Good branch managers develop their employees. They try them out on different tasks, attempting to broaden their skills. As those skills become more effective, a good branch manager looks for opportunities to enhance that employee's career path. As part of this trait, good managers are picky about who they hire or are given by the personnel department. A good manager has an objective of always hiring someone who could be better than himself. That is not threatening for a good manager. Good prodders possess excellent follow-through.

The fourth trait is that good branch managers have high energy levels. They hustle; that was the word we heard the most. They physically move around fast. They are on the move a lot. They do not procrastinate. They handle the hard problems first, literally diving into them and are eager to solve them. This is not an undisciplined loose cannon, yet it could be if the energy was not controlled.

Good branch managers set very high standards for themselves. Along with these personal standards comes the related process of setting high standards for the employees, as well as the branch itself. These branch managers always set sales goals on the high side and push the staff to a fault. They are careful not to be unrealistic with their goals, but the fact that they can sell and do the operational tasks allows them to be realistic.

Good branch managers are innovative: clever and creative in stretching the limits of their authority. Sometimes this trait gets them in trouble, but there is a saying that proves more often valuable than detrimental: *It is easier to apologize than to ask for permission.* Trying new things or doing old things in a new way is risky, but the rewards are greater (or far lesser) than following a proven low-risk pattern. Many employees are motivated and stimulated by new concepts.

On the other side of the management-attribute coin are characteristics of less-effective managers such as:

1. Low employee involvement
2. Management by intimidation
3. Unwillingness to accept new ideas, methods, or processes
4. Don't fix it if it isn't broken

Experience, hands-on communications, and involvement are the real burning issues for good managers. The era of the impersonal non-communicator sitting in his office is long gone. It has become a job of human resource understanding, development, and sensitivity.

Are you part of this movement? Are you grasping for change or wallowing in priorities? The task for the nineties is clear: control expenses and increase income. That means multiskilling ourselves and our staffs, creating high-performance teams within the branches, making suggestions to management, being a proud part of a team, and accepting the new role of sales into the bosom of the branch culture.

S U M M A R Y

1. Leadership has a lot to do with change. Management has a lot to do with priorities.

2. *Managers*   *Leaders*
   Plan and budget   Set directions
   Organize and staff   Align personnel
   Control and solve problems   Motivate and inspire

3. The tasks of goal setting, strategies, organization charts, and job specs are the natural tendencies of managers.

4. The tasks of ideas, vision statements, objectives, changing strategies, risk taking, and exploring are the natural tendencies of leaders.

5. Six distinct traits of good branch managers:
   a. Experienced
   b. Multiskilled
   c. Good prodders
   d. High energy levels
   e. High standards
   f. Innovative

6. Four characteristics of less-effective branch managers:
   a. Low employee involvement
   b. Management by intimidation
   c. Unwillingness to accept new ideas, methods, or processes
   d. Don't fix it if it isn't broken

CHAPTER 14

Discussing Case Studies

In this chapter we discuss the three case studies in the book and give solutions for each.

The first case is King's Kamera. The actual case study is found in Chapter 10, as is the case of Lee Advertising. Both deal with how a small business makes money and how to notice different aspects of a business to help you make sound banking decisions while soliciting small business accounts.

The third case is Posey County Bank and Trust. This case deals with management and sales management techniques used by branch managers.

There is little value to presenting a case study followed immediately by the discussion and solutions. Therefore, it is best to read the study carefully within the context of the chapter. Try to answer the questions at the end of the study. Once you have gone as far as you feel comfortable, then this chapter should be used. References to the exact page numbers and chapters are indicated where necessary. Naturally, there are few exact answers to cases, since subjectivity plays such a large part in the evaluations. My conclusions and the aggregate input of others who have participated in the cases represent the discussion solution section of each case.

I would appreciate further input or ideas to make these cases more accurate and would, therefore, suggest you contact me through the publisher.

KING'S KAMERA DISCUSSION

King's Kamera has proven to be a very valuable case study. It represents some very accurate numbers and management activity for the small, family business. The lessons learned from this case could easily apply to the other family-owned retail businesses.

The one overriding issue in this case that is allowed to continue is the fact that Delores should have sold something quickly, then come back using cross selling to build the relationship. As interesting as the sales chase appeared to be, it would be Delores's undoing. A good salesperson does not put everything in one bag and try to sell everything at once.

The recommended strategy for an account such as King's would be to get that first account for the bank! It is much easier to sell other products once the customer is used to doing business with you. So as admirable as it was for Delores to be chasing the Kings around, I would have recommended that Delores spend her energies focusing on some kind of sweep account that Mike and Delores clearly need. An account of this type would make money for them and those are the kinds of words Dorothy likes to hear.

I would question Delores's pursuit of the account via Mike. Even though Mike appears to be the more innovative of the two, Dorothy clearly controls the purse. So it would seem that the thrust of the sales effort would be to spend more time with Dorothy. Naturally, part of this time would be an education process, because Dorothy might be too focused and unwilling to look at new financing alternatives. The best example of this would be her reluctance to purchase the building. Even though they would be saving money and building equity, Dorothy will probably resist that step until she had figured out a way to save up for it. At that point, the property would be long gone.

Cultivating and nourishing a personality like Dorothy's is difficult. Her main thrust would be the family. Because of her personality, she ends up making all the major decisions. That is the role she has assigned herself. From a psychological point of view, that appears to be the role that Mike as assigned to her also. That should make the sale of other banking products very easy: concentrate on Dorothy. A favorite adage of mine is "Don't sell to the monkey; sell to the organ grinder." Dorothy is the organ grinder.

Selling Dorothy will take a longer time than Mike, because she will be more suspicious and needs more hand holding. If you can clearly see and understand the benefits of your banking products, then your customer (Dorothy) should also be able to see them, and purchase them.

Over a two-year period, Delores should have developed the following products or services:

1. Sweep account
2. Corporate savings instruments
3. Direct deposit
4. Employee checking/savings
5. Individual retirement account (or equivalent)
6. Equity line of credit
7. Commercial mortgage
8. Related insurance
9. Commercial loan

(If you are a banker in the United Kingdom, Ireland, or Europe, you could add travel services and total life and health insurance.) This account would be a profitable account for the bank due to the Kings' prudent financial approach and total commitment to a business.

In the process of developing this case study, bankers have asked many questions that are similar. I have attempted to answer those specific questions as simply as possible.

Answers to Questions Regarding King's Kamera

Q1. *Is it an advantage for a business like King's to employ members of the family? Why? Why not?*

A. There is an advantage for a family retail business to hire members of the family in that it controls hiring and turnover. The sooner the Kings can get their children into the business, the better. The labor market is tough. Training costs are often too high, and therefore, we put people into the workforce who are untrained. That negates the one piece of research we have that shows the major reason why people buy cameras (remember?): "professional, competent employees."

Q2. *What is the single largest expense in a retail business like King's? List it as a percentage of sales.*

A. The biggest expense in the business should be payroll. If King's payroll is $72,000 on $480,000 of sales, it is fairly on target. A good rule of thumb is 17 percent of sales should be payroll. Incidentally, this is true of many retail businesses.

Q3. *What is co-op advertising? Does it apply in this case?*

A. Camera dealers usually receive an advertising allowance from their suppliers of approximately 3 percent, as long as they put in an additional 3 percent. That's called co-op advertising.

Q4. *What is the gross margin at King's Kamera?*

A. 39 percent.

The following are fairly open-ended questions for you to think about. They are subjective in nature. My answers are just my answers, subjective and based on my style.

Q5. *How is King's Kamera doing? Is it making any money?*

A. Actually, King's is doing very well! From a banking point of view, King's appears to have all of their numbers in order and would make excellent customer both on the asset side and liability side.

Q6. *What kinds of things should the Kings be doing to improve their margin and strengthen their business?*

A. It would appear that Dorothy has her fingers into the margin based on her analysis of paying bills on time. The strengthening of the business will come from film processing, even a separate film-processing outlet. Additionally, owning their building would strengthen their business foundation by providing equity as well as (rental) income.

Q7. *If all salaries (except Mike's and Dorothy's) are $36,000, can they afford to pay themselves $36,000?*

A. Easily. Look at the bottom line. They have a profit of $35,000 that is going to be taxed unless they either pay the employees a bonus or themselves more salary.

Q8. *Do you believe that $72,000 as 47 percent of its total operating expense is too high? Why?*

A. As long as they can show a profit with their payroll at 48 percent, it is not too high. No matter how you look at it, all aspects of the payroll seem to be in perspective; that is, the Kings' salary plus everyone else.

Q9. *Should they buy the building? Why? How?*

A. Without any other information available. I would strongly recommend that they pursue negotiations with the building owners. They have an established location for their business and now an opportunity to own that established location. Financially they are sound both personally and businesswise. They could use their home to provide the size of the down payment they would need and probably not pay any more in mortgage payments than they are in rent. If the down payment was not too large for them to handle with their existing salaries, they do have some room to give themselves a raise.

Q10. *What banking products and services would encompass a reasonable full-service banking relationship?*

A. (1) Sweep account, (2) corporate savings instruments, (3) direct deposit, (4) employee checking/savings, (5) individual retirement account (or equivalent), (6) equity line of credit, (7) commercial mortgage, (8) related insurance, and (9) commercial loan.

LEE ADVERTISING DISCUSSION

Marilee's small business is on the fence for a branch manager in its size and complexity as a corporate account. A small branch would not want to get involved with an advertising agency of this size. Any ad agency with more than three- or four-persons would create problems for $20 million branch.

The major area of concern is that advertising is a very different kind of business. It relies to a large degree, on creative, volatile personnel. The risks are great, as are the rewards. In tight economic times, businesses chop their advertising budgets immediately. Even though, from a prudent business point of view, we know that when times are tough, one must be more aggressive in the pursuit of sales, American businesses cut their advertising budget at the hint of an economic slowdown. That makes the advertising business particularly sensitive to business climates. From a lending point of view, that should be a red flag unless the agency is well established and has weathered a couple of economic storms.

Small advertising agencies do make good deposit customers. Any lending should be heavily collateralized. A complex relationship should be avoided for the branch manager. Perhaps, Dan should have turned the entire account over to the commercial division and only stayed involved as an information funnel or liaison. The fact that Marilee was pushing Dan to move fast could mean that she had something to hide or that some creditors were pushing her and her cash flow was not handling her payables adequately. Never be pushed into an emotional loan or recommendation. You should always move at a pace that is comfortable for you. It is one thing to be a good salesperson, but it is more than the products or services that you sell that make money for the bank. Take your time. Never lose control of the sale. Let's review the numbers that Marilee has provided. She says her billings are $8 million and her income is $1.5 million. Mathematically, we can determine that her income is within an acceptable range, 18+ percent.

We should deduct her new business expense right off the top; $300,000 seems like a lot. Now we know her adjusted income is $1.2 million, or closer to 16 percent. We know that 50 percent of that should be for salaries ($600,000). If you take $200,000 from that for her two heavyweights, you have $400,000 for 10 salaries. That comes to $40,000 each. That isn't a lot of money, especially if Marilee is paying herself a salary.

One very important thing Dan should do is to see her cash flow. Service companies are more cash-flow sensitive than manufacturers. It appears she is looking for $10,000 per month for additional salaries. If you have done your numbers correctly, you can see that she does have a $300,000 gross profit. Assuming she can generate the cash flow, she should be able to afford the new people without borrowing. I would be suspicious about what she needs the money for.

Here are Dan's figures:

$1,500,000	sales
$750,000	salaries
$450,000	operating expenses
$300,000	gross profit

The good side of the customer equation is her assets: her $500,000 inherited home (no mortgage) and living quarters. She probably has around $700,000 in equity. If she is serious about her business, she could apply for an equity line of credit. If her salary is within suitable ranges, she probably would get the loan.

The big question with this prospective client is that because of the intricacies of equity and salaries and the size of the dollars, it might be best left to a commercial or corporate banker rather than a retail banker.

Answers to Questions Regarding Lee Advertising

Q1. *As Dan Wilson, what are the first five steps you are going to take with regard to preparing for the pursuit of Lee Advertising?*

A. *a.* Need to know Lee Advertising's cash flow.

b. Need full financial records prepared by an accountant.

c. Need to learn more about the advertising business. Maybe the consultant she hired would be willing to spend some time.

d. Need to see a business plan.

e. Need to talk to some references.

Q2. *Simply explained, what is the gross margin in an advertising agency?*

A. 100 percent of the money that comes in the door that is used for expenses and profits.

Q3. *Just from the information provided to this point, how would you loan money to Marilee?*

A. Very well collateralized loan via her personal real estate.

Q4. *What is her monthly payroll?*

A. $62,500.

Q5. *What is the income from a $8 million agency?*

A. Hypothetically, it is 20 percent, or $1.6 million.

Q6. *What is the income from an $8 million bank?*

A. It is almost impossible to determine. Here is a rough guess: around 3.5 percent, or $280,000.

Q7. *Draw an organization chart for the top three levels of a small $5–8 million advertising agency.*

A.

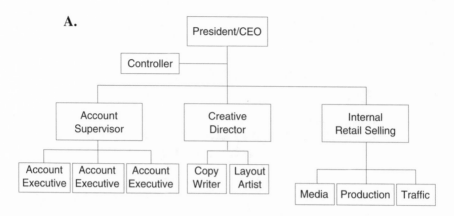

Q8. *What is Marilee's primary banking need in terms of product?*

A. A good line of credit to help with cash flow and a banker who is available constantly.

POSEY COUNTY BANK AND TRUST DISCUSSION

This case study reveals the complexities and stresses associated with managing a branch. My 25 years of working with branch managers have led to me believe that the Posey County Bank and Trust case study is not an exaggeration. Managing a branch in today's competitive environment is very stressful and requires some astute management skills.

Use the worksheet in on page 199 to assist you in visualizing this case study. Think about the case study briefly. Internalize in your mind the stress that Donna is under. Is it more than yours or less? How so? What are Donna's opportunities? How are they different than yours? Is this case study realistic from your point of view? How does it differ?

Answers to Questions Regarding Posey County Bank and Trust

Q1. *What is the size of Donna's branch in deposits?*

A. If you go back to page 16, you will see that based on the number of employees she has, her branch is probably around $35 to $40 million. Then page 166 will show you relative ratios and average second account new money.

Posey County Bank and Trust Worksheet

Think about the case study briefly. Internalize in your mind the stress that Donna is under. Is it more than yours or less?

How so?

What are Donna's opportunities?

How are they different than yours?

Is this case study realistic from your point of view? How does it differ?

Q2. *What is John Paine's ratio?*

A. You will have to make a carefully calculated guess. We know that Donna can keep up with John when she has a 1.73 ratio. So we could assume that he does have a 1.73 ratio. The chart on page 16 confirms that a branch that size could possibly have one salesperson doing that kind of cross selling.

Q3. *If John is responsible for 80 percent of the branch's second account cross-sold money. what do you suppose Minnie Jo is selling?*

A. First, let's look at John's second account new money figure. I would estimate it at 80 percent of $70,000, or $56,000. So if John has a ratio of 1.72 and is doing $56,000, then Minnie Jo at 1.25 probably has just about all of the rest.

Q4. *What is Minnie Jo's ratio?*

A. If she earned $50 in sales compensation and the CSRs are paid on the basis of $2 per hundredth of a cross-sell point, then we could safely assume she is selling at 1.25.

Q5. *What is Madeline's ratio?*

A. On page 159, I described luck as 1.10.

Q6. *What is the total of nonsalary sales compensation in the branch?*

A. John at $144, Minnie Jo at $50, and Madeline at $20. Tellers receive $175 in referrals and there is a $25 mystery shopper winner every month. That totals $414.

Q7. *How is Donna going to motivate Minnie Jo?*

A. Donna will motivate Minnie Jo through a structured schedule of coaching and allowing her to go to different sales seminars and meet other sales personnel within the bank. Slowly, Minnie Jo will come around.

Q8. *Should Donna be selling more? If so, what can she sacrifice?*

A. She might consider reassessing her operational responsibilities. When she replaces John, and she has to, she should get someone who could be promoted to assistant branch manager. A branch her size could use an assistant.

Q9. *If you were Arch Turner, what would you need to know about your branches?*

A. *a.* Is there a suitable physical sales environment?

b. Is the staff knowledgeable about the difference between selling and marketing?

c. Is there a steady pattern of growth in second account new money?

d. Is the merchandising and POS suitable to control and direct the branch traffic?

e. How is the morale in the branches?

f. Do the branch managers get involved with their staffs?

INDEX

Other books of interest to you from Irwin Professional Publishing . . .

Relationship Banking

Cross-Selling the Bank's Products and Services to Meet Your Customer's Every Financial Need
Dwight S. Ritter

Relationship Banking is an action plan for developing the customer base by offering customers value, not pressure. Natural opportunities for cross-selling are identified and solutions are offered for the inevitable staff and customer objections. Your existing staff and product line are used more effectively and profitably. 225 pages ISBN: 1–55738–381–2 $37.50

Reinventing the Retail Bank

Cross-Marketing Investment Products to Create the Full-Service Financial Center
Lawrence S. Harb & Sarah E. Sleight

The competitive financial services market demands that bankers be better informed on the products and services that they—and their competitors—offer. *Reinventing the Retail Bank* gives bankers the tools needed to make informed decisions and strategic choices that are right for them. The market demands that a full-service bank bring Wall Street to Main Street. *Reinventing the Retail Bank* shows you the smart way to do it. 300 pages ISBN: 1–55738–386–3 $47.50

The Bank Marketing Handbook

A Step-By-Step Guide for Today's Market-Driven Banker
R. Eric Reidenbach

With *The Bank Marketing Handbook,* any banker can become an informed marketer, from executive management to the head of retail operations. The easy-to-use workbook format can help you create, implement and manage a winning marketing program. *The Bank Marketing Handbook* encompasses the entire marketing realm, not just selling. This handbook is a hands-on approach to developing and running successful marketing plans. It effectively demystifies the marketing process for financial professionals. 175 pages ISBN: P 1–55738–7136–3 $49.95